SHIPBUILDING CONTRACT

"When things go south"

by

David Seah
LLB London

We are all apprentices in a craft
where no one ever becomes a master
- Ernest Hemingway-

Written and Published By
David N F Seah, LLB London

Published 2024

DISCLAIMER

THIS BOOK IS BASED ON THE PERSONAL RESEARCH AND OPINION OF THE AUTHOR AND IS MEANT FOR EDUCATIONAL PURPOSE ONLY. THE INFORMATION IN THE BOOK IS NOT INTENDED TO PROVIDE LEGAL ADVICE AND MUST NOT BE TREATED AS A SUBSTITUTE FOR SPECIFIC LEGAL ADVICE OR RELIED UPON UNDER ANY CIRCUMSTANCES.

THE AUTHOR AND PUBLISHER DOES NOT GUARANTEE THE ACCURACY OF THE INFORMATION IN THE BOOK AND HEREBY DISCLAIM RESPONSIBILITY FOR ANY LOSSES OR DAMAGES WHATSOEVER INCURRED THROUGH THE USE OF INFORMATION IN THIS BOOK.

BY PROCEEDING TO READ THIS BOOK, YOU IRREVOCABLY CONFIRM THAT YOU HAVE READ, UNDERSTOOD, AND ACCEPTED THE TERMS AND CONDITIONS IN THIS DISCLAIMER.

Dedicated to
Serene, Ivan, and Melissa

Introductory notes

Shipbuilding is a highly litigious industry with perennial disputes and things can go south from the initial negotiation when one party alleges that a binding contract or letter of intent (LOI) have been reached, but the other party disagrees. Even when the contract and LOI is binding, they may still be challenged for non-fulfilment of contingent conditions or on other grounds.

Production disputes: Throughout the production phase, disputes may revolve around plans, drawings, variations, over-inspection, workmanship, and the quality of the vessel. After sea trials, the buyer may allege that the vessel did not conform to the contract specification or performance criteria.

Delays: In the event of delayed delivery, the buyer may be entitled to liquidated damages. In such instance, the shipbuilder may allege that the liquidated damages provisions are void. In the event of excessive delays, the buyer could terminate the contract after a drop-dead date. However, shipbuilder may argue that the buyer calculated the drop-dead date incorrectly, as some of the delays were due to the buyer's default. Thus, the buyer wrongfully repudiated the contract.

Indemnity: Claims to relief under knock-for-knock provisions for property damage and personal injury may be disputed on the grounds that the provisions do not apply to negligence or wilful misconduct.

Delivery: Conflicts at this stage, may include the buyer's refusal to accept the vessel. After the vessel has been delivered, disputes may involve the finality of the protocol of delivery and acceptance, and the validity of warranty claims. There may also be disputes on liability for defects discovered after the warranty period had expired.

Other disputes: These may often include issues with consequential loss, financial cap on total liability, assignment, novation, title, termination for convenience, confidentiality, intellectual property, and insurance. Also, some of the issues during arbitration or litigation could include, among other things, allegations that:

- The contract was wrongfully repudiated.
- Termination for delays was wrongful.
- The time limit for arbitration has expired.
- The expert determination is wrong.
- The refund or payment guarantee is not enforceable.
- The accrued instalments are not payable.
- Consequential losses were explicitly excluded.
- Buyer had no title to uninstalled materials.

The preceding provides a preview of what this book has in store. For readers keen in exploring further, the subsequent chapters of the book cover nearly a hundred answers to general and legal issues in shipbuilding contracts, as well as cases on how the English courts decide shipbuilding disputes and associated matters.

Content

Cases

Acronyms

AC	Appeal Court
ARRC	Autonomous Rescue and Recovery Craft
AWES	Association of West European Shipbuilders
BIMCO NBC	Bimco Newbuildcon
BRI	Builder's Risk Insurance
CoA	Court of Appeal
Comm	Commercial Court
EWCA	England and Wales Court of Appeal
EWHC	England and Wales High Court
HL	House of Lords
HVAC	Heating, ventilation, and air conditioning
ILU	Institute of London Clauses for Builders' Risks
LJ	Lord Justice
LR	Lloyd's Reports
KB	Court of King's Bench Division
MR	Master of the Rolls
NSF	Norwegian Standard Form
QB	High Court Queens Bench division
SOGA	UK Sale of Goods Act 1979
SAJ	Shipbuilders Association of Japan
SSGA	Sale and Supply of Goods Act 1994
TCC	Technology and Construction Court
UKSC	United Kingdom Supreme Court
WLR	Weekly Law Report

Introduction

1. What is a shipbuilding contract?

A shipbuilding contract[1] is an agreement where the shipbuilder agrees to design, construct, equip, and deliver a ship to a buyer by a contractual delivery date. In return, the buyer agrees to pay the contract price promptly and accept the ship on the delivery date. The contract comprises the terms and conditions of agreement, as well as attachments.

Terms and conditions of agreement

Preamble	Guarantee
Recital	Tax
The Vessel	Plans and Drawings
Description	Planned Programme
Quality Standard	Buyer's Supplies
Implied Terms	Subcontractors
Classification	Variations
Financial	Tests and Trials
Contract Price	Delivery of the Vessel

[1] *See shipbuilding contract checklist, infra.*

Payment Terms	Health & Safety
Liquidated Damages	Confidentiality
Permissible Delays	Assignment
Cap on Total Liability	Intellectual Property Rights
Consequential Loss	Termination Rights
Indemnity	Governing Law
Insurance	Dispute Resolution
Warranty	Notice
Title	General Clauses

Attachments

Specification & Drawings	Buyer Supplies
Planned Programme	List of Approved Vendors
Progress Report (PR)	Shipyard Schedule of Rates
Payment Terms	Builder's Certificate
Payment Guarantee	Bill of Sale
Parent Company Guarantee	Protocol of Delivery and Acceptance
Insurances	Waiver of Liens and Claims
Variation Procedure	

Where a shipbuilding contract between parties from different countries is governed by English law, the contract will be an international supply contract under Section 26(2) UCTA[2].

Under the UCTA, a contract is an international supply contract if (a) it is a contract for the sale of goods (or one under which possession or ownership of goods passes, e.g., a contract for hire) made between parties whose places of business are in different States, and (b) the goods will be carried from the territory of one State to another; or the acts constituting offer and acceptance are done in the territories of different States; or the contract provides for the goods to be delivered to the territory of a State other than that within whose territory those acts were done.[3]

[2] *Unfair Contract Terms Act 1977.*
[3] *S24(4) UCTA.*

2. Why is the nature of a shipbuilding contract important?

Shipbuilding contracts governed by English law were previously treated as contracts for the sale of goods[4], and have also been considered akin to building contract or a contract for work and materials. More recently, the House of Lords have construed such contracts as one for the sale of a ship where the design and construction of the vessel formed part of the shipyard's contractual duties, as well as the duty to transfer the finished object to the buyer.

The legal effect of this on a shipbuilder's accrued right to unpaid instalment following lawful rescission of the contract, and issues on total failure of consideration was considered by the House of Lords in *Hyundai Heavy Industries v Papadopoulos.*[5] In the said case, the buyer defaulted in paying the second instalment. Consequently, the shipbuilder rescinded the contract and sued the buyer's guarantors to recover the second instalment. The guarantors argued that since the shipbuilder had rescinded the contract, the shipbuilder's right to reclaim the unpaid second instalment was cancelled, as the buyer's obligation was to pay damages. As damages were not covered by their guarantee, the guarantors contended that they were not liable.

The House of Lords held that the shipbuilder's accrued rights to the second instalment was payable by the guarantors. Viscount Dilhorne stated that the contract was not simply one for the sale of goods, but a contract to build, launch, equip, complete, deliver and sell the vessel. According to Lord Fraser, "...the shipbuilding contract has little similarity with a contract of sale and much more similarity, so far as the present issues are concerned, with contracts in which the party entitled to be paid had either performed work or provided

---

[4] *Behnkev Bede Shipping 1972 1KB 649.*
[5] *[1980] 1 WLR 1129 (HL).*

services for which payment is due by the date of cancellation. In contracts of the latter class, which of course includes building and construction contracts, accrued rights to payment are not (in the absence of express provisions) destroyed by cancellation of the contract."

Some years later, in the case of *Stocznia Gdanska SA v Latvian Shipping Co and Others*[6], concerning six shipbuilding contracts, each for the construction of single refrigerated or reefer vessels, the shipbuilder rescinded the contracts and claim for recovery of accrued instalments. However, the buyers argued that the shipbuilder was not entitled to the instalments. The buyers reasoned that if the instalments were paid, the buyers could recover it immediately as there been a total failure of consideration, i.e., the buyers have received nothing under the contract because no property in the vessel or any part was transferred to them. According to the buyers, the relevant question which the court should consider was whether the buyers have received the benefit of any part of that which they had bargained for. The court held that the question was not whether property in the vessel or any part of it passed to the buyers. Such a question would be appropriate if the contract was for the sale of goods or the sale of land. The question should be whether the shipbuilding contract in question was (a) simply a contract for the sale of a ship or (b) a contract under which the design and construction of the vessel formed part of the shipyard's contractual duties, as well as the duty to transfer the finished object to the buyers. The court concluded that it was the latter. As the construction of the vessel was in progress before the rescission of the contracts and there had been no total failure of consideration, the buyer was liable for the unpaid instalments.

---

[6] *[1998] UKHL 9; [1998] 1 All ER 883; [1998] 1 WLR 574.*

3. What constitutes a binding shipbuilding contract?

Parties to a potential shipbuilding project may often conduct pre-contract negotiation by in-person meeting or through electronic means (telephone, telex, or email). In the latter case, there could be disputes when one of the parties alleges that a binding contract has been reached, but the other party contended otherwise.

In the case of *Okura & Co Ltd v Navara Shipping Corp SA*[7], the parties entered into a contract for the construction and sale of a ship. Buyer cancelled the contract because of delays. Subsequently, the parties negotiated a new contract by telephone calls and telex. A memorandum of agreement (MOA) reflecting the terms in the telex was drafted but the buyer included additional terms that were inconsistent with those in the telex. The shipbuilder rejected these additional terms and the MOA was never signed. During the trial, the buyer maintained that there was a binding contract which was wrongfully repudiated by the shipbuilder, but the shipbuilder contended that there was no binding contract.

The judge of first instance, Neill J decided that there was a binding agreement between the parties as all essential terms had been agreed and the signing of a written memorandum of agreement was not a condition precedent to the formation of a binding contract. Also, since the shipbuilder subsequently repudiated the agreement, this ended the contract. On appeal, the CoA disagree and held that no agreement was concluded. Lord Denning MR stated that: "Everything was provisional only. The parties were not to be bound unless and until they signed an agreement ... Item 11 of the telex clearly contemplated that there should be a memorandum of agreement in mutually acceptable terms ... The telex itself was not binding. It was a preliminary to a future document which was to be binding when signed. The future document was drafted but it was never signed. It was never agreed by the parties."

---

[7] *[1982] 2 Lloyd's Rep 537. (CA).*

However, the outcome will be different if all the terms of the sale were agreed, and the signing of a memorandum of agreement was not a prerequisite to a binding contract. In *Damon Compania Naviera SA v Hapag-Lloyd International SA*[8], the sale of three ships from the seller to two brothers was negotiated by their respective brokers. The main terms of the memorandum of agreement (MOA), which incorporated the Norwegian Saleform with a sale price, were finalized through the exchange of telexes.

Under the MOA the buyer had to pay a deposit of 10% of the purchase money on signing the contract, The seller had the right to cancel the MOA if monies were not paid in accordance with the MOA; forfeit the deposit and claim compensation for any loss and for all expenses together with a 5% annual interest. As intended, the brothers novated the MOA to a Panamanian company. The brothers could lawfully negotiate and conclude contracts on the company's behalf as they were the directors, chairman and treasurer of the company. The existence of the agreement was acknowledged in subsequent telexes sent on the brothers' behalf. Despite the seller's request, no MOA was signed, nor the deposit paid. Consequently, the seller withdrew from the contract and sued the buyer. During arbitration, the arbitrator concluded that the agreement was binding and not subject to contract because the parties' brokers were satisfied that there was a concluded contract between their principals; and the agreement was regarded in the shipping market as a binding contract not requiring a signed memorandum to validate it.

The buyer's appeal was dismissed by the CoA. Fox LJ stated that even though contemplated, the execution of the memorandum of agreement was not a prerequisite to a binding contract as all the terms of the sale were agreed. The CoA also held that payment of the deposit was not a condition precedent to the formation of a contract but a

---

[8] *[1985] 1 Lloyd's Reports 93 (CA).*

fundamental term of the contract which had been concluded with the intention of substituting the buyers by a novation. As a result of the novation and the subsequent ratification of the contract, the parties have reached a binding contract.

It should be noted that although the cases above were decided on a different set of facts, the principles of construction remain the same. According to Lord Clarke in *RTS Flexible Systems Ltd v Molkerei Alois Muller GmbH & Co KG*[9], the question whether a contract is binding on the parties will not depend on the subjective intent of the parties, but rather, on their words or conduct, and whether it can be objectively concluded that they intended to enter into legal relation, and have agreed to all the terms they regarded or the law requires for forming a relationship that was legally binding.

In *Pagnan SPA and Feed Products Ltd*[10], Lloyd LJ summarized the principles (which were cited with approval by the UKSC in *RTS Flexible Systems Ltd v Molkerei Alois Muller GmbH*[11] as follows:

- To determine whether a contract has been concluded during correspondence, one must first look to the correspondence.
- Even if the parties have reached agreement on all the terms of the proposed contract, nevertheless they may intend that the contract shall not become binding until some further condition has been fulfilled. That is the ordinary 'subject to contract' case.
- Alternatively, they may intend that the contract shall not become binding until some further term or terms have been agreed.
- Conversely, the parties may intend to be bound forthwith even though there are further terms still to be agreed or some further

[9] *[2010] UKSC 14, Per Lord Clarke at 45.*
[10] *Pagnan SPA v Feed Products Ltd [1987] 2 Lloyd's Rep 601.*
[11] *[2010] UKSC 14, see letter of Intent, infra.*

formality to be fulfilled.

- If the parties fail to reach agreement on such further terms, the existing contract is not invalidated unless the failure to reach agreement on such further terms renders the contract unworkable or void for uncertainty.
- It is sometimes said that the parties must agree on the essential terms and it is only matters of detail which can be left over. This may be misleading, since the word 'essential' in that context is ambiguous. If by 'essential' one means a term without which the contract cannot be enforced then the statement is true: the law cannot enforce an incomplete contract. If by 'essential' one means a term which the parties have agreed to be essential for the formation of a binding contract, then the statement is tautologous. If by 'essential' one means only a term which the Court regards as important as opposed to a term which the Court regards as less important or a matter of detail, the statement is untrue. It is for the parties to decide whether they wish to be bound and if so, by what terms, whether important or unimportant. It is the parties who are, in the memorable phrase coined by the Judge [at page 611] 'the masters of their contractual fate'. Of course, the more important the term is the less likely it is that the parties will have left it for future decision. But there is no legal obstacle which stands in the way of the parties agreeing to be bound now while deferring important matters to be agreed later. It happens... when parties enter into so-called 'heads of agreement.

Contingent conditions

4. What is an effective date of contract provision?

Some contracts may provide for the signed contract to become effective only on the date when stipulated condition precedent are are fulfilled. See Article 16 of the AWES, which provides that: "This CONTRACT shall become effective the day after all the following conditions has been fulfilled: The Purchaser and Contractor shall notify each other in writing, which may bc by telefax if confirmed by letter, of the fulfilment of the above conditions. Should any of the above conditions not be fulfilled within ... Days from the date of signature of this CONTRACT, this CONTRACT shall not become effective and shall be regarded as never entered into; in such case no obligations whatever shall remain between the parties".

Also, in *Haugland Tankers v RMK Marine*,[12], concerning an option agreement, the exercise of an option was vitiated when the buyer failed to comply with the condition precedent for the valid exercise of the option.; namely to pay the commitment fee when exercising the option. Conversely, a condition subsequent arises when the parties agree that the contract is effective upon signing, but will become null and void if certain conditions after contract signing are not fulfilled by specified date. See *example in* SAJ Article *XIX, which* provides that*:* "The Contract shall be effective as from the date of

---

[12] *[2005] EWHC 321 (Comm).*

execution … However, in the event that a Construction permit for the Vessel shall not have been granted by the Japanese Government within (…) days from the date of this Contract, …then this Contract shall automatically become null and void, unless otherwise mutually agreed in writing."

In *Covington Marine Corporation v Xiamen Shipbuilding*[13], involving the construction of four bulk carriers, the effective date of contract was subject to a number of condition subsequent. One of the conditions stipulated that there had to be an agreement between the parties as to the supplier of the main engine within ten banking days from the date of the contract. After contract signing, the parties communicated via letters about the identity of the supplier of the main engine. Two of these letters were dated 18 and 19 March 2003 respectively. However, communication between the parties could not progress further after builder failed to reply to buyer's letter of 19 March 2003. It also transpires that on the date in question, the builder had agreed to build three of the same vessels for another buyer.

The buyers began arbitration proceedings against the builder for repudiatory breach of contract. One of the issues was whether the parties had reached the requisite agreement on the main engine supplier. Buyer contended that the requisite agreement was achieved by exchange of letters dated 18 and 19 March 2003, between the party's brokers. The builders raised jurisdiction issues and denied any binding contracts were concluded.

The arbitrators concluded that (a) the binding effect of the contracts depended on the party's agreement to the supplier of the main engines; and (b) the said letters 18 and 19 March 2003 did not contain any final agreement on the supplier of the main engines but was only "tentative and provisional". Thus, the contracts were automatically rescinded, and the issue of repudiation did not arise. On

13 *[2005] EWHC 2912 (Comm).*

appeal, the judge, Mr Justice Langley held that there was an agreement[14] on the supplier of the main engines and the arbitrators' decision was wrong in law. In doing so, he concluded, in respect to the letter of 18 March, that: "If it was not intended to make or to be read as making alternative offers open to acceptance in relation to the source and cost of the main engine it is difficult to understand what other purpose was to be served by what was said;". Further he added that the 19 March letter was "... phrased in terms of acceptance and not further negotiation as regards the main engine. An objective reader would ... readily conclude that there was agreement on the main engine...."

5. Can a party benefit from their own breach?

An important principle under English law is that neither party to a contract can benefit from their own breach of its terms. In *New Zealand Shipping Co. Ltd v Société des Atelier et Chantiers de France*[15], the contract stipulated that the ship had to be completed by a certain date, unless delayed by unpreventable causes, and that the contract would become void if thc builders failed or was unable to deliver the ship within eight months from the agreed date, except in the event of France becoming engaged in the European war, when the delivery date would be extended equal to the duration of the war, but not exceeding 18 months. As a result of France's participation in the European war, the builders were prevented from completing the vessel by unpreventable causes beyond their control. On the expiry of the said 18 months, the issue was whether the builders could treat the contract as null and void, even though the purchasers still require the builders to complete and deliver the vessel. The purchasers argued that the contract was only voidable at their option. The House of Lords held that the contract was void and not merely voidable at the option

---

[14] *The Judge also commented obiter that it was "....an agreement to agree" and that "It would not be a wrong or a breach of duty not to agree on the supplier of the main engine..."*
[15] *(1919) A.C. 1.*

of the purchaser. Also, as the avoidance of the contract were not due to the wrongful act or default of the builders, the builders were not precluded from alleging that the contract was void.

However, subsequent cases[16] have shown that the principle is one of construction and not law. Thus, its application can be excluded by the terms of a contract. Also, if the circumstances that caused the contract cancellation is not a breach of obligation owed by one party to the other, the former may rely upon the non-fulfilment of condition subsequent to avoid performance of his contractual obligation.

In *Fast Ferries One S.A v Ferries Australia Pty Ltd*[17], the shipbuilding contract for a fast catamarans was subject to Debis (finance company), agreeing to finance the vessel's construction on terms acceptable to the buyer and builder. The contract also stipulated that if the buyer satisfies all the requirements in the commitment letter, but Debis did not agree to provide the financing, this will not constitute a default by the buyer. In such a case, the deposit will be returned to the buyer and the contract deemed cancelled.

Negotiations between the builder, buyer, and Debis reached a stage where Debis issued a commitment letter subject to certain conditions. At this point, it was common ground that the contract was effective, and from the buyer's perspective, subject to a condition subsequent, namely the approval of Debis Credit Committee. However, further negotiations were aborted because of disagreements over new requirements from Debis and the builder. The buyer requested for the return of deposit paid to the builder plus half the cost thereof. The builder refused to return the deposit and contended among other things, that the buyer was in breach of implied term to

---

[16] *Gyllenhammar & Partners International Ltd and others v Sour Brodogradevna Industrija [1989] 2 Lloyd's Rep 403. Cheall v Association of Professional Executive Clerical and Computer Staff [1983] 2 A.C 180. Thompson v ASDA-MFI plc [1988] 1 Ch. 241.*
[17] *[2000] Lloyd's Rep 534.*

take reasonable steps and best endeavours to reach agreement with Debis, regardless of whether such requirements were stipulated in the commitment letter.

The court held that as the buyer was not in breach of any conditions, the non-fulfilment of condition subsequent terminates the contract. Thus, the deposit must be returned to the buyer.

According to David Steel J:

"… the parties were agreed on the "finance terms" the only outstanding matter was the need for credit committee approval which was perceive as being no more than a formality. While a term could readily be implied that neither party would prevent approval being given on the terms offered (e.g., by withdrawing the application) there is no basis (let alone necessity) for implying any term to the effect that either party was under an obligation to accept different financial terms."

Letter of intent

6. What is the purpose and legal effect of a letter of intent?

In shipbuilding projects, letter of intent is often used as prelude to the formation of a formal contract. Such letter of intent may stipulate that the parties will enter a formal contract after certain conditions are fulfilled; or the buyer's bid for a shipbuilding project is successful; or where the parties intend to bid for a project jointly.

Besides securing the shipbuilder's commitment for slot space, such letter of intent are useful when the parties are waiting for the finalization of financing, guarantees, or buyer's board approval. In addition, shipbuilders may also have to sign letters of intent with subcontractors and suppliers in anticipation of a formal agreement for work or service to support potential shipbuilding projects.

7. What are the legal principles governing a letter of intent?

In *ERDC Group v Brunel University*[18], it was said that the phrase 'letter of intent' is not a term of art, as its legal effect will depend on the circumstances of each case; the communications

---

[18] *ERDC Group v Brunel University [2006] EWHC 687 (TCC).*

between the parties; and their actions[19].

If a letter of intent is qualified by the rubric "subject to contract", there will be no binding contract until a written contract is signed. In *Star Steamship Society v Beogradska Plovidba (The Junior K)* [20], it was held that the effect of the phrase was to prevent any contract being concluded until all of the terms had been agreed. However, it is also possible for an agreement which is 'subject to contract' or 'subject to written contract' to become legally binding if the parties later agree to waive such conditions[21]. The parties may also agree to bind themselves to agreed terms, leaving certain subsidiary and legally inessential terms to be decided later.

In *Pagnan SPA v Feed Products Ltd*,[22] it was held that although certain terms of economic significance to the parties were not agreed, neither party intended that agreement of those terms to be a precondition to a concluded agreement. The parties regarded them as relatively minor details which could be sorted out without difficulty once a bargain was struck. Thus, the parties could bind themselves to agreed terms, leaving certain subsidiary and legally inessential terms to be decided later.

Where the scope of work has been identified, the parties may agree that they will not be bound unless their board's approval are obtained. In such a case, it has been held that the parties are not bound until their respective board approval are obtained.[23]

If an agreement is "subject" to some event(s) it will likely be a

---

[19] *Tesco Stores v Costain Construction [2003] EWHC 1487 (TCC), per HHJ Richard Seymour QC at para [160], and also RTS Flexible Systems Ltd v Molkerei Alois Muller GmbH [2010] UKSC 14, at para 45.*

[20] *[1988] 2 Lloyd's Rep 583.*

[21] *RTS Flexible Systems Ltd v Molkerei Alois Muller GmbH. [2010] UKSC 14, infra.*

[22] *[1987] 2 Lloyd's Rep 60.*

[23] *Windschuegl (Charles H) Ltd v Pickering & Co Ltd (1950) 84 Ll LR 89, 92).*

precondition rather than a performance condition[24] where:

- The fulfilment of the subject involves the exercise of a personal or commercial judgment by one of the putative contracting parties (e.g., as to whether that party is satisfied with the outcome of a survey or as to the terms on which it wishes to contract with any third-party).
- Such event can only be resolved by one or both of the parties removing or lifting the subject, rather than occurring automatically on the occurrence of some external event such as the granting of a permission or licence.

8. What is the peril of starting work based on a letter of intent?

Disputes may often arise where one party starts work based on a letter of intent, but before concluding the final contract. The perils of such a position are highlighted in the two cases below. Even though not related to shipbuilding, the principles are equally applicable.

Case 1: In *RTS Flexible Systems Ltd v Molkerei Alois Muller GmbH & Co. KG*[25], RTS and Muller signed a letter of intent ("LOI") for provision of work and equipment to automate Muller's product re-packaging process. The terms of the LOI provided that:

- RTS shall build, deliver, complete, install, and commission certain equipment for Muller.
- The agreed price was GBP 1,682,000.
- RTS shall begin all work and supply by a certain date.
- The final contract (based on Muller's amended form of MF/1 contract) shall be finalised and signed within 4 weeks of the LOI.

---

24 *Nautica Marine Limited v Trafigura Trading LLC [2020] EWHC 1986 (Comm).*
25 *[2010] UKSC 14.*

While negotiations were ongoing, but before the terms of the final contract were agreed, RTS started work based on the LOI. The LOI expired on 27 May 2005. The final version of the contract was agreed in the e-mail exchanges of 19 and 25 May, 29 June, and 5 July 2005. Though ready for execution, the contract was never signed. Subsequently, problems arose, and this led to a variation of the delivery plans on 25 August 2005. In the litigation that follows, RTS asserted that there was a continuing contract on the terms of the LOI. Alternatively, if there was no contract, RTS was entitled to a quantum meruit, or if there was a contract, that was on MF/1 terms. Müller's case was that there was a contract on the basis that Müller would pay the price, namely £1,682,000, in return for the goods and services that RTS had agreed to provide.

On appeal, the UK Supreme Court (UKSC) had to decide whether there was a contract between the parties after the expiry of the LOI and, if so, the terms thereof. The UKSC noted the perils of parties agreeing that work should proceed before a formal written contract is executed, and also commented that the "moral of the story is to agree to terms first and start work later".

The UKSC unanimously held that the parties reached a binding agreement on or about 25 August 2005 on the terms agreed by 5 July (as subsequently varied on 25 August), and that the binding agreement was not subject to contract. According to the UKSC, it was possible for an agreement which is subject to contract, written or otherwise, to become binding if the parties later agree to waive that condition. On or by 25 August, the parties had agreed to waive the "subject to contract" provision. Any other conclusion makes no commercial sense. In arriving at its decision, the UKSC also stated, inter alia, that in order to consider whether a contract is binding the court will have to examine the parties' words and conduct, to objectively conclude whether they intended to create legal relations and had agreed upon all the terms which they regard, or the law requires as essential for the formation of legally binding relations. Even where certain terms of economic or other significance were not finalized, an objective review of their words and conduct may show that such terms were not a precondition to a binding and legally enforceable agreement.

Case 2: In *Arcadis Consulting (UK) Ltd v AMEC (BCS) Ltd*26, AMEC engaged Acardis to carry out certain design works for a car park in anticipation of a formal protocol agreement that did not materialize. The relevant correspondences between the parties were as follows:

8 November 2001: Email with attachments comprising a Protocol Agreement, in the form of an umbrella agreement for design work to be performed by Arcadis on two projects: (1) Wellcome Building and (2) Castlepoint Car Park. The attachments included Condition 2A, which limit Arcadis' liability for defective work to the lesser of (a) “The reasonable direct costs of repair, renewal and/or reinstatement of any part or part of the Sub-Contract Works to the extent that the Client [AMEC] incurs such costs...”; or (b) “The sum stated in Schedule 1”, which was left blank. (the “November Terms”).

January 2002: New terms, including a proposed limit of liability in the sum of £110,000 were introduced (“the January terms”).

6 March 2002: AMEC letter instructing Arcadis to start work on the Castlepoint Car Park project, "to be carried out in accordance to the Protocol Agreement and Terms and Conditions associated that we [AMEC] are currently working under with yourselves" (the “First Letter of 6 March”).

6 March 2002: AMEC’s second letter of 6 March 2002 with schedules,

---

[26] *[2018] EWCA Civ 2222.*

which includes a proposed limit on Arcadis' liability to £610,515.

The car park was defective and would have to be demolished and rebuilt at about £40 million, including damages. Arcadis denied liability and also argued that if they were liable, their contractual liability was capped at £610, 515. AMEC argued that there was no contract as the correspondence envisaged a final contract, and such a contract was never finalized,

Coulson J, at first instance, decided that (1) there was a simple contract resulting from AMEC's first letter of 6 March 2002, as evidenced by Arcadis's conduct in undertaking the work; (2) Acardis never accepted the November Terms, or they had been superseded; (3) the phrase "the terms and conditions we are currently working under with yourselves" in the first letter of 6 March refers to the terms which were still being negotiated; (4) the cap on liability did not apply as the Protocol Agreement was not concluded, and there was uncertainty on whether the parties intended to be bound by such a cap.

However, the Court of Appeal (CoA) held that there was an interim contract where Acardis was performing work, and a final contract or Protocol Agreement, which would supersede the interim contract once agreed upon.

According to the CoA, a contract had been formed by the first letter of 06 March 2002 and the November Terms were the agreed terms referred to and incorporated by reference into it. The phrase "currently working under" refers to the November Terms the parties had previously exchanged and agreed to work under. Thus, the cap on liability under Condition 2A (a) of the November Terms applies to the interim contract.

In so doing, Dame Elizabeth Gloster (with whom Lord Justice

Holroyde and Lord Justice Underhill concurred) considers Goff J's analysis in *British Steel Corp v Cleveland Bridge & Engineering Co Ltd*[27], that if the parties are in a stage of negotiation and one party asks the other to begin work pending the parties entering into a formal contract, it cannot be inferred from the other party acting on that request that he is assuming any responsibility for his performance, except such responsibility as will be assumed under the terms of the contract that both parties are confident will be shortly finalized.

---

27 *[1984] 1 All ER 504.*

Option Agreement

9. What is the purpose of an option agreement?

Occasionally, a shipbuilder may agree that in addition to the vessel to be built under a contract, the buyer will have an option to purchase additional vessel(s).

The terms of such an option could either be incorporated as part of a shipbuilding contract or a separate option agreement. In the latter case, the terms and conditions of the option agreement will have to stipulate the following:

- The type of vessel, its dimensions, and particulars.
- The specification, equipment, and class notation.
- The contract price of the option vessel(s).
- The delivery date of the option vessel(s).
- The deadline for exercising the option, and contingent conditions (i.e., together with payment of deposit).
- The form of shipbuilding contract, which will usually be in substantially identical form, mutatis mutandis to the shipbuilding contract under which the option is granted.
- The deadline to finalise and sign the shipbuilding contract.

10. What is necessary for the valid exercise of an option?

This will include strict compliance with conditions stipulated in the option. In *Haugland Tankers v RMK Marine*,[28] the term of an option agreement provided that the buyer could exercise the option by the service of notice together with payment of a commitment fee to seller. The buyer served notice to declare the option but did not pay the commitment fee. It was held that simultaneous payment of the commitment fee was a condition precedent to or a requirement for the proper exercise of the option.

11. What happens when an option and the contract conflicts?

In *Ravennavi S.p.A. v New Century Shipbuilding Co. Ltd*[29], the shipyard granted the buyer an option to purchase two more vessels, for delivery by certain dates, and upon the terms of a previous shipbuilding contract, as amended by the terms of the option. The option also provided that if there are any possible earlier delivery for the two vessels, then the shipbuilder will grant the buyer or its nominee such earlier delivery date.

About a month after the exercise of the option, the parties signed two new shipbuilding contracts, with terms similar to a previous shipbuilding contract, save for the price, delivery dates and specific amendments to payment security. The new shipbuilding contracts did not include any term about possible earlier delivery for the two vessels. It also included an entire agreement clause. Subsequently, the buyer discovered that the shipyard was offering to build vessel for third party with delivery date earlier than those set out in the option.

---

[28] *[2005] EWHC 321 (Comm).*
[29] *2007] EWCA Civ 58.*

The central issue was whether the shipyard's obligation in the option concerning the earlier delivery date, would continue to exist after the option has been exercised, despite the signing of a formal shipbuilding contract which make no mention of any such obligation and contain an entire agreement clause.

The CoA unanimously held that the parties intended that the shipyard should offer the buyer an earlier delivery date if one became available prior to the exercise of the option. However, once the option had been exercised, the delivery date would be fixed once and for all.

12. Is an option with no delivery date void for uncertainty?

Delivery dates in an option agreement was once again the focus of dispute in *Teekay Tankers Ltd v STX Offshore & Shipbuilding Co. Ltd*[30]. The shipbuilder and buyer concluded an option agreement for three additional sets of up to four vessels. The option agreement specified the form and content of the shipbuilding contracts, the dates for exercising the options, the contract price, and the specification of the vessels. The delivery dates for each of the option vessels was to be mutually agreed at the time the buyer declared the relevant option. It was also agreed that the shipbuilder will make best efforts to have delivery within 2016 for each of the first optional vessels, within 2017 for each of the second optional vessels, and within 2017 for each of the third optional vessels.

After the buyer had exercised the option for the optional vessels, the shipbuilder could not proceed further with the transaction due to difficulties in procuring refund guarantees.

The buyer alleged that the shipbuilder had repudiated the option agreement and proceeded to cancel the agreement and claim damages.

---

30 *[2017] EWHC 253 (Comm).*

However, the shipbuilder denied liability and argued that the option agreement was void for uncertainty, and alternatively, that it has neither repudiated nor renounced the option agreement. The buyer disagrees and argued that:

- The delivery date in respect of each optional vessel was to be mutually agreed.
- Otherwise, the delivery date in respect of each optional vessel was to be such date as the shipbuilder offered, having used its best efforts to provide a delivery date within 2016 (for the first optional vessels) or 2017 (for the second and third optional vessels.
- If shipbuilder was unable to offer a date within the relevant year, despite its best efforts, the earliest date thereafter which shipbuilder was able to offer, and
- Alternatively, it was an implied term that the delivery date in respect of each optional vessel was to be an objectively reasonable date (having regard to shipbuilder's obligation to use its best efforts to provide delivery dates within 2016 or 2017 as appropriate).

The court held that the option agreement was void for uncertainty for the following reasons:

- If the buyer's argument were to prevail, this would mean implying a term where the shipbuilder could declare a delivery date unilaterally, thus the delivery date would not be mutually agreed.
- As for the objective reasonableness argument, the Judge held that this would be inconsistent with the phrase "will make best efforts" because the parties' position on what would be deemed a 'reasonable' delivery date will be different.
- There is a crucial distinction between agreeing to use best efforts

or best endeavours (a) to achieve a particular result, and (b) to reach agreement upon an essential term in a contract.

- There was no protocol on how the parties should seek to reach mutual agreement on delivery dates.
- If the buyer did not seek a delivery date within the relevant year, then there would be no need for the shipbuilder to consider offering a delivery date within that year.
- Should the buyer seek a date within the relevant year, then the shipbuilder could use its best efforts, at least to provide a date within the year, if not the date which buyer sought.
- Moreover, the buyer is at liberty, in its own interests, to reject any date provided by the shipbuilder.
- The words "best efforts" is just part of a process of seeking to agree upon an essential term in the relevant shipbuilding contracts. This was very "different from valid and enforceable obligations to use best efforts to achieve a result."

Plans and drawings

13. What is the purpose of a plans and drawings (P&D) provision?

Under such a provision, the shipbuilder will have to submit P&D for the buyer's approval. While the purpose for the transmittal of P&D will be omitted from most contracts, it is apparent that during the process, buyer will have an opportunity to identify shortcomings for variation, early rectification or to propose a better solution. In addition to obligating shipbuilder to submit P&D, the P&D provision[31] will specify the following:

- State the time for shipbuilder to submit P&D for buyer's approval.
- Legislate the timeframe for P&D transmittals between the parties.
- Elucidate the consequence of the buyer's late return of the P&D or failure to return the same.
- Guide the parties on the steps to take, if the buyer's comments on the P&D are vague or ambiguous, or the shipbuilder considers the buyer's comment to be a variation.

---

[31] *See AWES, Article 2(b), Bimco NEWBUILDCON, Clause 20(b), NSF, Article V.1 (a). SAJ, Article IV(1)(a).*

- Clarifies the effect of the buyer's approval or non-approval of such P&D.

The final paragraph in P&D provisions may provide that the buyer's approval of plans and drawings will not diminish the shipbuilder's obligations for errors, omissions, or shipbuilder's obligations under the contract. Also, where the contract provides that the buyer's approval of plans and drawings shall not affect the parties' obligation, shipbuilder may be precluded from asserting a defence of estoppel[32]. Salient example:

"The Buyer's approval or deemed approval of any plans and drawings shall not affect the obligations of the Builder to design, construct and deliver, or the obligations of the Buyer to take delivery of, and pay for, the vessel in accordance with the other provisions of this Contract, nor shall it diminish the Builder's responsibility in respect of its obligation under this Contract nor shall it constitute any acceptance by the Buyer of any responsibility for any defect in the Vessel." See Bimco NBC, cl 20(f).

14. Is the buyer liable for the late return of plans and drawings?

Most shipbuilding contracts will provide that if buyer fails to return the plans and drawings by a stated period or at all, the plans and drawings will be regarded as approved[33]; deemed approved by the buyer; or considered as approved[34]; or deemed to be automatically approved without comment by the buyer. Thus, in such cases, buyer will not be liable for failure to return the plans and drawings. See also,

---

[32] *Cenargo Ltd v Empresa Nacional Bazan de Construcciones Navales Militares SA [2001] EWHC 543 (QB), [2002] EXCA Civ 524 QBD (Comm).*

[33] *AWES Article 2 (b) The drawings and technical information shall be regarded as approved.*

[34] *NSF Article VI (d) Builder shall have the right to consider such plans and drawings as approved by Buyer. See also: Bimco NBC Clause 20 (e)...Plans and Drawings shall be deemed to have been approved by the Buyer.*

Zhoushan Jinhaiwan v Golden Exquisite Inc & 2 others[35], infra, where it was held that the buyer was not liable for late return or approval of procedures and drawings as (a) the vessel's specifications were all agreed and annexed to the contracts; and (b) there was no contractual obligation for the buyer's supervisor's approval to be sought or obtained for any procedures or drawings.

15. Who is liable for design errors?

In general, the shipbuilder will be responsible for the design of the vessel if they assume contractual liability for the design (partial or complete); the contract is silent on design responsibility[36]; or where the shipbuilder agrees to verify the adequacy of the buyer's design without any qualifications. The buyer will be responsible for design error if they provided the design[37], or shipbuilder expressly excludes liability for design responsibility. Where the shipbuilder assumes liability for buyer's partially developed design or agrees to verify the buyer's design, especially for prototype vessel, the contract may provide that:

- The buyer or its designer grants to shipbuilder, at no cost, such licence to use the design for the construction and sale of the vessel to buyer.
- The costs of verification are for buyer's account.
- The buyer should remain liable for consequences of design error that exist prior to date of design handover to shipbuilder.
- The buyer will indemnify the shipbuilder against all claims for

---

35 *[2014] EWHC 4050 (Comm).*
36 *Aktiebolaget Gotaverken v Westminster Corporation of Monrovia and another [1971] 2 Lloyd's Report 505.*
37 *Dixen Kerly Ltd v Robinson [1965] 2 Lloyd's Rep. 404.*

infringement of third-party intellectual property rights associated with the design provided by the buyer.

Also, if the design of a shipbuilder's subcontractor is defective, the shipbuilder will be liable to buyer if the contract is silent on the matter; and/or if the contract provides that the shipbuilder shall remain solely responsible for the proper performance of any subcontract works as if undertaken by the shipbuilder. See also industry standard form shipbuilding contracts:

Bimco NBC, cl 19, paragraph 2: Notwithstanding any sub-contracting, the Builder shall remain fully responsible for the due performance of such works as if undertaken by the Builder at the shipyard.

NSF cl 4, paragraph 1: The Builder shall remain fully liable for the due performance of such work as if done by the Builder at the Builder's yard.

SAJ Article 1.4: The Builder may, at its sole discretion and responsibility, subcontract any portion of the construction work of the vessel.

Variation

16. What is the purpose of a variation clause?

While contract amendment deals with fundamental changes to a contract, the right to modify the specification, drawings or work scope in shipbuilding contracts are usually stipulated in a variation clause. Such variations may be buyer-initiated, shipbuilder-initiated or due to changes in classification society rules and regulations.

Buyer-initiated variation may include the addition or deletion of the work; modification of specification, drawings; and acceleration of the work at its own expense. It should be noted that in some contracts, the shipbuilder is only obligated to carry out buyer's variation request if the shipbuilder construction program is not adversely affected in relation to its other commitments, and the buyer agrees to compensate the shipbuilder for costs and time impact.

Shipbuilder-initiated variation may include minor changes to the specification or work scope; delays due to buyer's default or excluded delays; extension of time for suspension of work due to late payment of instalments by the buyer and changes in classification rules declared after the date of contract signing.

17. What is not a variation?

When a proposed variation is outside the scope of the contract, the shipbuilder is not obligated to carry out the variation and may treat it as a request to enter a new contract.

In *Blue Circle Industries Plc v Holland Dredging Co (UK) Limited*[38], regarding a dredging contract, the contractor was asked to use materials from the dredging to create an island for a bird sanctuary. The parties had differing views on whether this was a variation. The court decided that the creation of the island was a separate contract and awarded the contractor the costs of carrying out the additional work. Other instances of what is not a variation include the following, where:

- Work or items are within the shipbuilder's work scope.
- Instruction for the shipbuilder to comply with its contractual obligations.
- The shipbuilder unilaterally carries out work not required in the contract or instructed by buyer,
- The shipbuilder supplies better quality material without the buyer's instruction.
- The shipbuilder undertakes acceleration or overtime work to mitigate its own delays.
- Where work is defined by reference to the specification and plans and the performance of necessary work is implicitly part of the shipbuilder's obligation even though they are not referred to in the specification.

---

38 *(1987) 37 BLR 40.*

18. What are the common terms in a variation provision?

In addition to the answers in question 17, such provision will state that all variation requests and orders must be in writing, and submitted for consideration or approval in a timely manner, and the following:

Pricing and payment terms: This will specify that all variations will be performed on a lump sum basis.

Disagreement on pricing: Where the parties cannot agree to a lump sum pricing, the provision may state that the variation shall be performed on unit or time and materials basis (T&M) per the shipbuilder's rates specified in the contract.

Material pricing: The provision may state that the price payable by the buyer for materials used in performing T&M work will be at shipbuilder's net cost plus an agreed percentage mark-up.
Payment terms: For variation performed on a lump sum basis this could be paid in two equal instalments; upon the signing of the variation order, and when the variation work is completed. Payment for variation work on unit or T&M basis could be monthly.

Deleted work: Where part of the work is deleted by the buyer, the provision may stipulate that (a) the shipbuilder must be compensated for the portion of work performed and all demobilization costs, including, it's committed or cancellation costs for materials and equipment ordered, and (b) deleted work cannot be offered to another contractor.

Variation order: The provision will also stipulate that information to be provided in variation order must include the following:

- The nature of change required.
- A statement of effect.
- Supporting documents.
- Lump sum price, unit or time and materials pricing.
- Payment terms.
- Total costs for the proposed variation.
- Breakdown of labour and materials costs.
- Changes in the scheduled delivery date.
- Any other relevant consequences caused by the variation.

19. What is the legal effect of a "no oral modification" clause?

Under English law the contracting parties are free to agree whatever terms they wish, and can do so in writing, orally or by conduct, or course of dealing.

However, if the contract comprised a "no oral modification" clause (NOM clause), what is the effect of non-compliance. In an earlier judicial decision, a "variations must be in writing" clause in a deed of guarantee prevented an oral agreement to vary the terms of the guarantee from taking effect.[39]

In *World Online Telecom v, I-Way Ltd*[40], the lower court and CoA refused to grant summary judgment and held that the "variations must be in writing" clause prevented an oral variation. At the subsequent full trial, the commercial court, held that the contract had been varied orally despite the "variations must be in writing" clause.

However, there appears to be a shift in judicial thinking, and according to the UKSC below if a contract comprised a "no oral modification" clause, oral variation will not be effective, save where

---

[39] *United Bank Ltd. v ASIF11.02.2000, unreported.*
[40] *[2002] EWCA Civ 413.*

estoppel is applicable. In *Rock Advertising Ltd v MWB Business Exchange Centres Ltd*[41], the UKSC had to decide on the effectiveness of an oral variation where the contract contains a no oral variation (NOM) clause. MWB and Rock entered into a licence agreement for Rock to occupy an office space for a fixed term of 12 months. Clause 7.6 of the agreement provided that:

"... All variations to this Licence must be agreed, set out in writing and signed on behalf of both parties before they take effect."

Subsequently, the licence fee was in arrears and Rock proposed a revised schedule of payments to defer certain payments with the arrears spread over the remainder of the licence term. A dispute arose as to whether Rock's proposal was accepted orally.

The judge of first instance found that that the variation was ineffective because it was not recorded in writing The CoA thought otherwise and held that the oral agreement to revise the schedule of payments amounted to an agreement to dispense with clause 7.6.

On appeal, the UKSC unanimously held that in the absence of writing and signatures as prescribed by clause 7.6 of the licence agreement the oral variation was invalid. Lord Sumption (with whom the majority agreed) stated, inter alia that:

"There are at least three reasons for including such clauses. The first is that it prevents attempts to undermine written agreements by informal means, a possibility which is open to abuse, for example in raising defences to summary judgment. Secondly, in circumstances where oral discussions can easily give rise to misunderstandings and crossed purposes, it avoids disputes not just about whether a variation was intended but also about its exact terms. Thirdly, a measure of formality in recording variations makes it easier for corporations to police internal rules restricting the authority to agree them."

---

[41] *[2018] UKSC 24.*

20. Can excessive variations frustrate a contract?

It has been held that where a contract contains a mechanism for addressing variations, substantial variation requests may not frustrate the contract. In *McAlpine Humberoak Ltd v McDermott International Inc*[42], McAlpine agreed to fabricate four pallets in connection with an oil rig for McDermott. The contract comprises a variation or change order clause detailing the procedure and price mechanism for McDermott-initiated variations. Delivery of the pallets were delayed and McAlpine attributed this to the numerous variation orders issued by McDermott. The court agreed with McAlpine contention that the contract has been frustrated and awarded McAlpine a quantum merit. On appeal, the CoA held that as the contract contains a mechanism for addressing variations, the contract was not frustrated.

In contrast, and to circumvent the effect of this ruling, some contracts[43] will limit the quantity of variation request to a reasonable amount, by words to the effect that buyer's variation request will be subject to shipbuilder's reasonable judgment that such variation does not adversely affect the shipbuilder's planning or program and other commitments. The latter is especially critical for freeing up slot space during period of high demand for newbuilding.

---

[42] *[1992] CILL 747.*

[43] *See AWES Article 3 (a), Bimco NBC Clause 24(b), NSF Article VI.1, and SAJ Article V.1.*

Liquidated damages

21. What are liquidated damages?

Liquidated damages are the predetermined estimate of loss to one party when the other party has delayed or failed to meet contract deadline or achieve certain performance criteria. Its purpose is to provide for adequate compensation to one party, while ensuring that the other party is not unreasonably penalized. If there are no liquidated damages provision or if such provision is construed as invalid, damages will be at large, and in the event of delays, buyer may be able to end the contract and claim for damages under common law.

In *Triple Point Technology Inc v PTT Public Company Ltd*[44], Lord Leggatt succinctly described the purpose of liquidated damages clauses in construction and engineering contracts as follows:

"... a clause in a contract which stipulates what amount of money will be payable as damages for loss caused by a breach of the contract irrespective of what loss may actually be suffered if a breach of the relevant kind (typically, delay in performance of the contract) occurs. Liquidated damages clauses are a standard feature of major construction and engineering contracts and commonly provide

---

[44] *[2021] UKSC 29, at Para 74.*

for damages to be payable at a specified rate for each week or day of delay in the completion of work by the contractor after the contractual completion date has passed. Such a clause serves two useful purposes. First, establishing what financial loss delay has caused the employer would often be an intractable task capable of giving rise to costly disputes. Fixing in advance the damages payable for such delay avoids such difficulty and cost. Second, such a clause limits the contractor's exposure to liability of an otherwise unknown and open-ended kind, while at the same time giving the employer certainty about the amount that it will be entitled to recover as compensation. Each party is therefore better able to manage the risk of delay in the completion of the project."

22. What is the purpose of liquidated damage clauses?

Under such clauses, a shipbuilder is liable for liquidated damages if the delivery of the vessel is delayed beyond the scheduled delivery date. Sample clause:

If the delivery of the vessel is delayed by more than 30 days beyond the delivery date due to non-permissible delay, then, in such event, beginning at twelve o'clock midnight on the 31st day after the delivery date, Shipbuilder shall be liable to pay the buyer by way of liquidated damages, and not as a penalty, the amount of [US$ insert amount] per day or part thereof, capped at 10% of the contract price. Such liquidated damages will not apply to any period of permissible delays.

There will usually be a grace period of about 30 days before the imposition of liquidated damages. The amount payable is commonly computed based on time (daily, weekly, or monthly) or a percentage of the contract price. Such provision will also provide that if the liquidated damages payable has reached its maximum cap, the buyer may cancel the contract.

Also, in some contracts, the shipbuilder may be liable for liquidated damages if the vessel's performance exceeds or is below its allowable margin, as illustrated in the table below.

Vessel Performance Criteria

Vessel Performance Allowable Margin				
Particular	Trial Speed	Fuel Consumption*	Net Cargo Capacity (100%)	Deck Cargo Area
Warranty	Min __ knots	___ gm/ kWh	___cubic metres	___ m²
Allowable Margin	___ knots deficiency	___ % of warranty	___% deficiency per itemised capacity	___% deficiency
LD for deficiency increase against allowable margin	US $ XXX per each further 0.1 knot deficiency	US $ XXX per each 1% increase	US $XXX for 1% of deficiency per itemised capacity	US $XXX per each 1% of deficiency
Maximum Excess or Deficiency	___ knots deficiency	5% of warranty	5% of overall capacity	5% deficiency

Such vessel performance excess or deficiency are determined during the inspection, tests and trials and sea trials of the vessel. The contract or specification will usually provide for sea trials to be conducted during favourable weather, under specific wind and sea conditions [i.e., wind speed not exceeding Beaufort Wind Force 3 and vessel at 4.0 metres draft as specified in the specification]. If the weather or draft conditions during sea trials differs from that of the contract specification, parties could agree that the speed trial be postponed or that adjustments be made by reference to the data obtained during model testing.

23. How are liquidated damages clauses construed?

Historically, the validity of liquidated damages provision will depend on whether such provision is construed by the courts to be a genuine pre-estimate of loss or void as a penalty.

In the case of *Dunlop Pneumatic Tyre Co Limited v New Garage and Motor Co Limited* [45], Lord Dunedin said that a provision would be penalty if (a) the stipulated sum is extravagant and unconscionable in amount in comparison with the greatest loss that could conceivably be proved to have followed from the breach; (b) that the provision would be penal if the breach consisted only in the non-payment of money and it provided for the payment of a larger sum; (c) that there was 'a presumption (but no more)' that it would be penal if it was payable in a number of events of varying gravity; and (d) that it would not be treated as penal by reason only of the impossibility of precisely pre-estimating the true loss. Subsequent to the *Dunlop Pneumatic v New Garage* case, the courts have held that a liquidated damages provision will not be a penalty if it is commercially justifiable, and its dominant purpose was not to deter the other party from breach.

In *Lordsvale Finance Plc v Bank of Zambia*[46], a provision in a syndicated loan agreement provides for interest to be paid at a higher rate during any period when the borrower was in default. Colman J decided that the clause was valid because its predominant purpose was

---

[45] *[1915] AC 79.*
[46] *1996] QB 752, 762, per Colman.*

not to deter default but to reflect the greater credit risk associated with a borrower in default. He also stated that there would seem to be:

> "...no reason in principle why a contractual provision the effect of which was to increase the consideration payable under an executory contract upon the happening of a default should be struck down as a penalty if the increase could in the circumstances be explained as commercially justifiable, provided always that its dominant purpose was not to deter the other party from breach."

Conversely, a liquidated damages clause will be held to be a penalty and unenforceable if the sum is extravagant, unconscionable, and a deterrence with no other commercial justification.

In *Unaoil Ltd v Leighton Offshore Pte Ltd*,[47] Unaoil and Leighton Offshore signed a Memorandum of Agreement (the JICA MOA), for a crude oil export facility reconstruction project. Under the terms of the JICA MOA, Unaoil was to be Leighton's subcontractor for the execution of onshore construction activities at an all-inclusive price of USD 75,000,000. Clause 8.1 provides that if Leighton's client awards the project to Leighton and Leighton breaches the terms of the MOA, Leighton shall pay to Unaoil liquidated damages amounting to USD 40,000,000. Later, the JICA MOA was amended by Supplementary Agreement 1 and 2. Under Supplementary Agreement 1, Article 2.7 of the JICA MOA was replaced with the following words:

> "Leighton Offshore and Unaoil agree a minimum price to be paid to Unaoil for construction and marketing of US$ 55,000,000 (fifty-five million US dollars".

However, although the price under the JICA MOA was reduced, the liquidated damages provision under Article 8.1 of the JICA MOA was not amended and liquidated damages payable remains at US$40

---

[47] *[2014] EWHC 2965 (Comm).*

million. In the ensuing dispute Unaoil submitted three claims, one of which was for liquidated damages of US$40 million per Article 8 of the JICA MOA. Elder J held that Article 8.1 of the JICA MOA is a penalty and unenforceable. In so doing he explained that:

- Whether a liquidated damages clause is a penalty should be viewed at the date of the contract, or the date of subsequent amendment.
- As the contract in the case before the court was amended in a relevant respect, the relevant date is the date of such amended contract.
- Since the original contract price was reduced, the liquidated damages of US$40 million was no longer a genuine pre-estimate of likely loss and was objectively "extravagant and unconscionable with a predominant function of deterrence" without any other commercial justification.

In *Azimut-Benetti SpA (Benetti Division) v Darrell Marcus Healey*[48], concerning a yacht construction contract, the High Court held that a liquidated damages clause in the contract was not a penalty and granted summary judgement in favour of the claimant. Azimut-Benetti SpA, a luxury yacht builder in Italy (claimant) had contracted to construct a 60-metre yacht for Shoreacres Ltd, (buyer) an Isle of Man special purpose company wholly owned by the defendant at a contract price of €38 million, payable by instalments. The scheduled delivery date was 30 November 2011. The defendant issued a personal guarantee. Clause 16 of the Yacht Construction Contract dated 25 September 2008 and in particular clause 16.3, provided as follows:

"16.1 In addition to such rights as it may have at general law the Builder may

[48] *[2010] EWHC 2234 (Comm).*

suspend construction of the Yacht and/or terminate this Contract at any time by written notice to the Buyer: (a) if the Buyer fails to pay any sum due and owing under this Contract within forty-five days after the due date; ... 16.3: Upon lawful termination of this Contract by the Builder it will be entitled to retain out of the payments made by the Buyer and/or recover from the Buyer an amount equal to 20% of the Contract Price by way of liquidated damages as compensation for its estimated losses (including agreed loss of profit) and subject to that retention the Builder will promptly return the balance of sums received from the Buyer together with the Buyer's Supplies if not yet installed in the Yacht."

The first instalment comprising 10% of the contract price was not paid. On 22 January 2010 the claimant terminated the contract and demanded payment of €7.1 million being 20% of the contract price of €38 million less €0.5 million paid by way of deposit. A demand for a similar sum was also issued against the defendant under his guarantee. The claimant applied for summary judgement against the defendant.

The defendant resisted the summary judgment claim by asserting that the liquidated damages in the contract with Shoreacres were a deterrent and a penalty. Thus, there is no liability under the guarantee. The defendant also relied on the presumption that it is a penalty in cases if a single lump sum is payable by way of compensation on the occurrence of one or more of several events, some of which may be serious and others trifling damage.

The claimant maintains that by the terms of the guarantee the guarantor is liable even if the clause is unenforceable, and the principal debtor is not, or that an estoppel arises. The claimant also has an alternative claim for the first instalment of the price which had fallen due under the contract at the time of termination. The defendant contended that having elected to sue on for liquidated damages, the claimant is not entitled to summary judgment for the first instalment.

The Judge agreed that defendant's submissions did not take account of the provisions of clause 16.3 as a whole as it places an obligation on the buyer, and also places an obligation on the claimant, to promptly return the balance of sums received from the buyer together with the buyer supplies if not yet installed in the Yacht. The claimant submitted that the evidence shows that clause 16.3 had a clear commercial and compensatory justification, and was not merely a liquidated damages clause, but provided for payments to the buyer also, was not a deterrent, and falls within these principles. The claimant also relied on the exchanges between the contracting parties where an alternative clause based on actual loss, but with the attendant possibility of considerable delay in reimbursement were proposed to the buyer. However, the buyer agreed to clause 16.3 as proposed by the builder.

The Judge held that the clause was not a deterrent but was commercially justifiable as providing a balance between the parties upon lawful termination by the builder.

He added that the contract was for the construction and sale of a very expensive yacht, aptly described in the evidence as a super-yacht. Each of the party had the benefit of expert representation in finalising the contract. The terms of the contract, including the liquidated damages clause, were freely entered. Therefore, the clause in question is not a penalty and is enforceable.

The Judge held that the claimant is entitled to summary judgment for €7.1 million being 20% of the contract price of €38 million less €0.5 million paid by way of deposit.

On the claimant's alternative claim for the first instalment, the Judge held that in view of his decision on the penalty point, this alternative claim does not arise. He noted in passing that if he had held that clause 16.3 was not enforceable, the claimant would be able to claim the first instalment citing the decision in *Hyundai Heavy Industries Co Ltd v Papadopoulos*[49] where on this question, a

[49] *[1980] 1 WLR 1129, HL.*

majority of the House of Lords held that the builder's right to the instalment was not affected by the termination of the shipbuilding contract.

In *Triple Point Technology v PTT Public Company*[50], which concerns the interpretation of liquidated damages clause in a Software Contract[51], Triple Point was obligated to design, install (by data transmission), maintain and licence software to assist PTT in carrying on its commodity trading business. The contract provided for liquidated damages to be paid in the event of the Triple Point's delay, calculated at a daily rate from the due date for delivery up to the date PTT accepts such work. There was also a cap on Triple Point's liability, but excluding both specific remedies identified in the contract, and liability for "fraud, negligence, gross negligence or wilful misconduct".

Subsequently, disputes arose between the parties. Triple Point demanded payment due on its invoices. PTT refused pay on the grounds that they were not payable under the terms of the Contract. Triple Point suspended performance and PTT terminated the contract.

The issues before the court of first instance were (a) whether liquidated damages were payable for work which had not been completed before the contract was terminated; and (2) the interpretation of an exception to a cap on the contractor's liability for damages when the liability results from negligence. The court held that PTT was entitled to liquidated damages for delays prior to termination. The CoA disagree, set aside the judge's award of liquidated damages, and held that PTT was only entitled to liquidated

---

50 *Triple Point Technology Inc v PTT Public Company Ltd [2021] UKSC 29.*

51 *The case is also of relevance to shipbuilder's agreements with its vendors for the supply and installation of automation, computerised systems, software, as such agreements will usually comprise liquidated damages clauses for delivery and performance delays.*

damages for delays in the completion of works that were accepted by PTT under Phase I, and not for liquidated damages under Phase 2 where the work was not completed or accepted by PTT. The UKSC unanimously allows PPT's appeal and held that the liquidated damages were applicable up to the date of termination.

Lady Arden pointed out that the decision in *British Glanzstoff Manufacturing Co Ltd v General Accident, Fire and Life Assurance Corporation Ltd* [52] to which the CoA had given significant importance, was confined to its specific facts and did not create a special rule applying to liquidated damages clauses. She added that CoA's departure from the generally understood meaning of liquidated damages clauses will be inconsistent with commercial reality and the accepted function of liquidated damages. In her view, it was:

"...unrealistic to interpret the clause as meaning that if that event does not occur the contractor is free from all liability for liquidated damages, and ... accrued right to liquidated damages simply disappears. It is much more probable ... for liquidated damages to cease on completion and acceptance of the works to stand in addition to and not in substitution for the right to liquidated damages down to termination. Reading the clause in that way meets commercial common sense and prevents the unlikely elimination of accrued rights."

Lord Leggatt agrees with Lady Arden that the appeal should be allowed for the reasons she gives and added his own reason for reaching such conclusion. He disagrees with the CoA's position that if Triple Point never completes the work because PTT terminates the contract lawfully, then there is no liability to pay liquidated damages. This will not be consistent with the language as the clause specifies the conditions that must be met for liability to pay liquidated damages to arise, and acceptance of the work by PTT is not one of them. He

---

[52] *[1913] AC 143.*

further said that: "...the clause clearly signifies that, ... the liability to pay the agreed sum for each day of delay will run from the due date of delivery and will go on running until the work is accepted. That is the effect of the clause, no more and no less. If the contract is terminated, the liability to pay liquidated damages stops running, not because the end date specified in the clause has been reached, but because Triple Point ceases to be under an obligation to deliver work with which it is failing to comply."

He concluded that the purpose of agreeing that a sum will be payable as liquidated damages for each day of delay caused by the contractor would be defeated if the stipulated sum was payable only when the contractor chose to complete the contract.

24. What is the true test for the validity of liquidated damages?

The UKSC revisited the penal rule recently and held that "The concepts of 'deterrence' and "genuine pre-estimate of loss" are unhelpful, and the true test is whether the impugned provision is a secondary obligation which imposes a detriment on the contract-breaker out of all proportion to any legitimate interest of the innocent party in the enforcement of the primary obligation."

In *Cavendish Square Holding BV v Talal El Makdessi* [53], Makdessi sold a controlling stake in a holding company to Cavendish. Under clause 5.1 of the contract, if Makdessi is in breach of certain restrictive covenants against competing activities, he will not be entitled to receive the final two instalments of the price, and under clause 5.6 of the contract, Makdessi could be required to sell his remaining shares to Cavendish, at a price which would excludes the value of the goodwill of the business. Makdessi breached these covenants and in the ensuing litigation, Makdessi contended that

---

[53] *[2015] UKSC 67.*

clauses 5.1 and 5.6 were unenforceable as penalty clauses.

In the court of first instance, Burton J held that the two provisions were valid and enforceable. This was overruled by the CoA which held that the clauses were unenforceable as a traditionally understood penalty. On appeal, the UKSC reviewed and set out the legal principles regarding the penalty rule as follows:

- The rule against penalties is a rule of contract law based on public policy and the courts will not enforce a stipulation for punishment for breach of contract.
- It is construed by construction of the parties' contract by reference to the circumstances at the time of contracting.
- The concepts of 'deterrence' and "genuine pre-estimate of loss" are unhelpful, and the true test is whether the impugned provision is a secondary obligation which imposes a detriment on the contract-breaker out of all proportion to any legitimate interest of the innocent party in the enforcement of the primary obligation.
- However, "if the contract does not impose (expressly or impliedly) an obligation to perform the act, but simply provides that, if one party does not perform, he will pay the other party a specified sum, the obligation to pay the specified sum is a conditional primary obligation and cannot be a penalty."
- The court will consider whether any (if so what) legitimate business interest is served and protected by the clause, and if so, whether the provision made for that interest is extravagant, exorbitant, or unconscionable.
- Where contracting parties are properly advised and of equal bargaining power, there is a strong initial presumption that the parties are the best judges of what is legitimate in a provision dealing with the consequences of a breach.

The UKSC reversed the decision of the CoA and held that clauses 5.1 and 5.6 did not impose secondary but primary obligations. Also, they were price adjustment clauses with legitimate function for Cavendish to achieve its commercial objective of acquiring the business and protecting its goodwill.

Delays and Extension of time

25. What are permissible and non-permissible delays?

One of the key obligations of a shipbuilder is to deliver the vessel by a scheduled delivery date. Thus, if a shipbuilder fails to deliver the vessel by such a date (or any valid extension thereto), there will be contractual consequences. The legal effect of such consequences will depend on whether the failure to deliver is due to permissible, non-permissible or excessive delay.

The term "permissible delay" will be interpreted according to the language used in the contract. Generally, this may include delays caused by force majeure events or excluded delays, or delays caused by the buyer's default as defined in the contract. In the former case, shipbuilder will have the right to extend the delivery date[54], and in the latter, shipbuilder may be compensated for time and cost impact.

Non-permissible delays, on the other hand refers to delay in the delivery of the vessel caused by the shipbuilder's default. In such an event, the shipbuilder will have to pay liquidated damage to the buyer. Where such liquidated damage exceeds a specified cap, usually 10% of the contract price, the buyer may terminate the contract.

---

[54] *Subject to a specified period, after which the contract may be terminated.*

In the case of *Zhoushan Jinhaiwan v Golden Exquisite Inc & 2 others*[55], which involved the proper construction of cancellation and delay clauses in four materially identical shipbuilding contracts, Leggatt J stated at paragraph 68 that: "… delays in construction are prima facie the responsibility of the Builder, unless they are excused by a provision of the contract. The basic default position under the contract, in other words, is that delay is "non-permissible" unless a term of the contract classifies it as permissible (or, in the case of excluded delays, deems it not to be delay at all)."

Article VIII.I of the contracts provide that the shipyard had the right to extend the delivery date if the shipyard is affected by a list of force majeure events.

Article VIII.I.4 defines permissible delay as: "Delays on account of such causes as provided for in Paragraph 1 of this Article excluding any other extensions of a nature which under the terms of this Contract permit postponement of the DELIVERY DATE, shall be understood to be (and are herein referred to as) "permissible" delays, and are to be distinguished from "non-permissible" delays on account of which the CONTRACT PRICE of the VESSEL is subject to adjustment as provided for in Article III hereof."

Article III.1(c) provides that the buyer could cancel the contract if the delivery of the vessel is delayed for a period of at least 210 days.

Article VIII.3 provides that the buyer could cancel the contract if the if the total of all accumulated permissible delays is 225 days or more, or the permissible and non-permissible delays collectively is 270 days or more.

---

55 *[2014] EWHC 4050 (Comm).*

Excluded delays did not counted as delays for the purpose of any right of cancellation as there was no contractual provision that state otherwise.

The buyer cancelled the contracts as the shipbuilder failed to deliver the vessels by the schedule delivery date and beyond 270 days thereafter. The shipyard alleged that the cancellation was wrongful as some of the delays was caused by buyer's own breach of contract which amounted to a repudiatory breach. However, notice of such breach was not given to buyer and the shipyard only made the claim for such breach after the contracts had been cancelled.

The shipyard argued that under Article IV, the buyer undertook and assured that its supervisor would carry out inspections "in accordance with the agreed inspection procedure and schedule and usual shipbuilding practice and in a way as to minimize any increase in building costs and delays in the construction of the VESSEL." However, the buyer's supervisor worked short hours and this delayed the inspection process. The supervisor also imposed unreasonable requirements beyond those specified in the contract, specification, class rules and regulations, agreed standards and general practices. All these delays the construction process. Also, the shipyard could not carry out further construction as the buyer's supervisor did not return the procedures or vessel drawings timely. According to the shipyard, such buyer's breach delays was the fourth category of delay.

The judge, Mr Leggatt J pointed out that the shipyard is only obliged to correct such nonconformity if it agrees with the buyer's supervisor, as the buyer's supervisor has no power to delay the construction of the vessel. If the supervisor points out what he thinks is a failure by the shipyard to build the vessel in accordance with the contract, shipyard could decide whether it agrees or disagrees with the supervisor. In the former case, shipyard must correct the defect, and in the latter case, shipyard is free to ignore the supervisor. Also, whilst the supervisor had the right to attend tests and carry out inspections, the shipyard was not contractually required to wait for him. Equally, if the supervisor sought to impose unreasonable requirements beyond those specified in the contract, the shipyard had no obligation to comply with them. As for the late return of procedures or drawings, the specifications for the vessel were all agreed and annexed to the contracts, and the contracts did not stipulate for the supervisor's approval to be sought or obtained for any procedures or drawings.

Ultimately, Leggatt J held that:

- The alleged delay caused by buyer's breach under Article IV were non-permissible delays, which could be included in (a) the period of 210 days' delay after the delivery date under Article III.1(c), and (b) the period of 270 days' delay under Article VIII.3; either of which entitles the buyer to terminate the contract.
- Even if the delays under Article IV were characterised as permissible delays, buyer could still cancel the contracts, as the delay in each case exceeded the length of time, giving rise to a right of cancellation under Article VIII.3.
- If (contrary to his view), the buyer's breach delays fall within the scope of Article VIII.1, the shipyard cannot claim that the delays were permissible delays as shipyard has failed to give notice as required under the contract.

26. What is the purpose of force majeure clauses?

The purpose of force majeure clause in shipbuilding contract is to suspend an affected party's delays or non-performance of the contract for a limited period if unforeseeable circumstances prevented such party from fulfilling their contractual duties. The term "force majeure" literally means "greater force" and the concept of force majeure which originated from French civil law has no fixed or recognized meaning under English law. Thus, what constitutes force majeure events must be expressly listed out in the contract. According to Male LJ[56], a typical force majeure clause will: "... lists a number of events or causes beyond the parties' control...defines the effect on a party's performance of the contract which such events must have if the clause is to apply; and...specifies the consequences on the parties' contractual responsibility when that occurs."

Thus, the elements of a force majeure clause in shipbuilding contracts will comprise the following:

- A list of force majeure events or circumstances, such as acts of God, governmental intervention, lockdowns, natural disasters, wars, epidemics, pandemics, strikes, fire etc. Such a list may be exhaustive or illustrative, depending on the wordings.
- The remedies available for the affected party, such as suspension, extension, termination, or relief of the contractual obligations for the party affected.
- The conditions and procedures for invoking the clause, such as notification, mitigation, and supporting evidence.

27. What constitutes a valid force majeure claim?

The question of whether relief under a force majeure clause can be successfully invoked will depend on the language of the clause. As Males LJ[57] puts it: "It is simply a matter of construing the words of the clause.... what matters is the language of the clause, the citation of cases dealing with very differently worded clauses is ... of limited if any assistance." Also in *Tandrin Aviation Holdings Ltd v Aero Toy*

---

[56] *Classic Maritime Holdings Inc v Limbugan Makmur SDN BHD, Lion Diversified Holdings BHD [2019] 4 All E.R. 1145, at paragraph 31.*
[57] *At paragraph 37 of the Classic Maritime v Limbugan's case.*

Store LLC[58], the commercial court said that force majeure is not a term of art and whether a force majeure clause in a contract is triggered will depend on the proper construction of the wording of that clause.

Regarding judicial interpretation of force majeure clauses, these are governed by the normal rules of construction, and certain general rules have been established by the English courts.

Notice provision

Most force majeure clauses will comprise notice provision that the affected party must notify the other party of any force majeure claim within a specified number of days, failing which the affected party will not be entitled to relief. Whether compliance with such notice provision is a condition precedent that validates the affected party's claim will depend on its wordings. In *Bremer Handelsgesellschaft mbH v Vanden Avenne-Izegem PVBA*[59], it was said that whether a notice provision is a condition precedent will depend upon three matters; the form of the clause itself, the relation of the clause to the contract as a whole, and the general consideration of law.

Burden of proof

The party claiming relief bears the burden of proof. *In Seadrill Ghana Operations Ltd v Tullow Ghana Limited,*[60], it was said that the party relying on a force majeure event to excuse the non-performance of its obligations bears the burden of proving on a balance of probabilities that there was nothing that it could reasonably have done to avoid or circumvent the force majeure event.

---

58 [2010] EWHC 40 (Comm).
59 Per Lord Wilberforce, A [1978] 2 Lloyd's Rep 109, 113.
60 [2018] EWHC 1640 (Comm), paragraph 97.

Duty to mitigate

Where the contract provides, a party claiming relief must show that the force majeure event is unforeseeable and beyond its reasonable control, and all reasonable endeavours or efforts has been taken to avoid or minimize the effects of such an occurrence.

It was held in *Channel Island Ferries Ltd v Sealink UK Ltd*[61], that "a party must not only bring himself within the clause but must show that he has taken all reasonable steps to avoid its operation or mitigate its results". The court have also held that the force majeure provision which include strikes 'beyond the control' of a party did not cover strikes that could be settled by taking reasonable steps to increase the crews' wages.

In *2 Entertain Video Ltd v Sony DADC Europe*[62], Sony provided logistics services, storage and distribution facilities at its warehouse for 2E and the other claimants. During the London riots in 2011, intruders entered and set fire to Sony's warehouse. 2E's stock with a sales value of about £40 million, stored in Sony's warehouse were destroyed. 2E claimed damages for the loss suffered. Sony argued that the events was unforeseeable and could not have been prevented by reasonable measures. The court held that the risks of unauthorised entry and arson were reasonably foreseeable and within Sony's reasonable control, but Sony failed to secure the warehouse adequately against such risks. Also, in *Seadrill Ghana Operations Limited v Tullow Ghana Limited*[63] Justice Teare said that:

"The reason why in the present context, a force majeure clause, the mere fact that a step is contrary to a party's commercial interests is insufficient to show that it has exercised it reasonable endeavours is that in such context the party

---

61 *[1998] 1 Lloyd's Rep 323, per Parker LJ (at 327).*
62 *[2020] EWHC 972 (TCC).*
63 *[2018] EWHC 1640 (Comm), at paragraph 94.*

cannot ignore the commercial interests of the other party in the force majeure being avoided or circumvented."

Ambiguous language

Where the language a force majeure clause is uncertain, this may vitiate the clause. In *British Electrical and Assocd. Industries (Cardiff) Ltd v Patley Pressings Ltd*, [64], a clause which states that the "usual 'force majeure' clauses shall apply" was held to be void for uncertainty.

The 'but for' test

A party cannot not rely on force majeure occurrence to avoid liability if it was never going to perform the contract in any event.

In the case of *Classic Maritime Inc v Limbungan Makmur Sdn Bhd*[65], a shipowner and charterers entered into a long-term contract of affreightment for shipments of iron ore pellets from Tubarao or Ponta Ubu in Brazil to Port Kelang or Labuan in Malaysia on tonnage to be provided by the shipowner. The charterer failed to carry out five shipments of cargoes between November 2015 and June 2016. On 5 November 2015, a dam burst and the iron ore mine which supplies iron ore pellets for shipment from Ponta Ubu had to stop production. During the litigation, the charterer sought to avoid liability for its failure to supply the five shipments of cargoes by relying on clause 32 of the contract, which provided as follows: "Neither the Vessel, her Master or Owners, nor the Charterers, Shippers or Receivers shall be responsible for loss or damage to, or failure to supply, load, discharge or deliver the cargo resulting from: Act of God… floods…; Landslips; accidents at the mine or Production facility...or any other causes beyond the Owners', Charterers', Shippers' or Receivers' Control; always provided that any such events directly affect the performance of either party under This Charter Party. If any time is lost due to such events or causes such time shall not count as Laytime or demurrage…"

---

[64] *[1953] 1 WLR. 280*

[65] *Classic Maritime Inc v Limbungan Makmur Sdn Bhd [2019] EWCA Civ 1102.*

The shipowner submitted that charterer must prove that, but for the dam burst, it could and would have performed the contract. The charterer asserted that while the clause did impose a causation requirement, the dam burst made any performance impossible. Thus, it did not have to prove that it could or would have performed the contract but for the force majeure event. The charterer cited the House of Lords' decision in *Bremer Handelsgesellschaft v Vanden*[66], a prohibition clause in the then current version of GAFTA 100, which established that it was not necessary for a party seeking to rely on force majeure to show that it would have performed its obligations but for the force majeure. The judge of first instance, Teare J found that although the dam burst rendered it impossible for the charterer to perform the five shipments, the charterer cannot rely upon the exception clause referring to "accidents at the mine" because it was not ready and willing to provide cargoes for shipment even if the dam burst had not occurred. However, the judge held that the shipowner was not entitled to recover substantial damages and awarded nominal damages of US $1 for each shipment.

On appeal, the CoA held that (a) the charterer could not rely on the dam burst to avoid liability "when it was never going to perform those shipments anyway" (b) the shipowner was entitled to damages of US $19,869,573 in respect of the five shipments. During the hearing, LJ Males, (with whom LJ Haddon-Cave and Lady Justice Rose agreed) stated inter alia that:

- It is preferable to concentrate on the terms of clause 32, as the citation of cases with differently worded clauses is of limited if any assistance.
- Clause 32 is a general exceptions clause of mutual application, which when invoked will exempt a party from responsibility for a

[66] *Bremer Handelsgesellschaft mbH. v Vanden Avenne-Izegem PVB [1978] 2 Lloyd's Rep 109.*

breach of an obligation, which includes "loss or damage to, or failure to supply, load, discharge or deliver the cargo".

- The combination of words like "resulting from" and "directly affect the performance of either party" import a causation requirement which were confirm by the word "any other causes" and "such events or causes."
- The dam burst and charterer's performance was not "directly affected" as the charterer had no intention of supplying any cargo.
- The words "loss or damage to cargo" refers to cargo which was in fact lost or damaged because of one or more of the events listed in the clause.
- The clause in the Bremer's case cited by the charterer was a contractual frustration" clause (Clause 21 of the GAFTA 100 form), which automatically discharged the parties from an obligation to perform in the future. Thus, it was not necessary to meet the "but for" causation test. In contrast, Clause 32 did not provide for an automatic cancellation of the contract (or of individual shipments) for the future.

Causal connection

Force majeure relief will avail if there is a causal connection between the force majeure event and the failure to perform.

In *Seadrill v Tullow* mentioned earlier, Justice Teare considered the contractual wording "if and to the extent that fulfilment has been delayed or temporarily prevented by an occurrence as hereunder defined as Force Majeure," and held that the language did not cover a situation where a party's failure to perform was caused by two matters, one a force majeure event, and the other not. Also, in *Coastal (Bermuda) Petroleum Ltd v VTT Vulcan Petroleum SA (No 2) (The Marine Star)*[67], a governmental authority's request to a party to a contract not to perform the contract was not covered by the force majeure clause

---

[67] *[1996] 2 Lloyd's Rep 383.*

because it was the affected party who initiated the request from the governmental authority.

Commercial impracticality

Force majeure relief for commercial impracticable will not be granted unless the parties effectively contracted to that effect.

In *Thames Valley Power Limited v Total Gas & Power Limited*[68], Thames Valley and Total entered into a Gas Supply Agreement (GSA) whereby Total agreed to supply gas to Thames for a 15-year period, less six days, from a date in the middle of 1995. Until 1st October 1997 the prices were to be fixed, although there was to be an increase after 1st June 1996. Clause 15.1 of the standard conditions releases a party affected by any force majeure event from its obligations and suspension of its rights to the extent to which they are affected by and for the duration of such force majeure event. Clause 15.2 defines the term force majeure as:

> "...any event or circumstances beyond the control of the party concerned resulting in the failure by that party in the fulfilment of any of its obligations under this agreement and which notwithstanding the exercise by it of reasonable diligence and foresight it was or would have been unable to prevent or overcome. ... it is acknowledged that any event or circumstance which qualifies as force majeure under the supplier's carriage agreement with British Gas shall be deemed to be a force majeure hereunder. In assessing the circumstances of force majeure affecting the customer, the price of gas under this agreement shall be excluded."

On 5th July 2005 Total served a force majeure notice under clause 15 that:

- It has become uneconomic to continue to supply gas to Thames under the Gas Supply Agreement.

---

68 *[2005] EWHC 2208 (Comm).*

- Unless there is a significant fall in the anticipated UK market price of gas during the autumn and winter months, TGP will be unable to carry out its obligation to supply gas after 30th September 2005 until further notice.
- During this period TGP would be willing to supply gas to TVPL at a bare "pass through" price."
- There will be a point when the market price becomes so high that it is commercially impracticable for TGP to continue.

In the trial that followed, Mr. Justice Clarke said inter alia, that Total's obligation to supply the gas in accordance with the contract is neither dependent on nor related to the market price of gas; and the fact that it is much more expensive does not mean that Total cannot do so. He also quoted an example from *Tennants Lancashire Limited v Wilson CS & Co Ltd* [69], where Lord Loriburn observed at p.510: "The argument that a man can be excused from performance of his contract when it becomes 'commercially impossible' seems to me to be a dangerous contention which ought not to be admitted unless the parties plainly contracted to that effect." Mr. Justice Clarke concluded that:

- Each clause must be considered on its own wording and that force majeure clauses are not to be interpreted on the assumption that they are necessarily intended to express in words the common law doctrine of frustration.
- Total was not entitled to serve the notice in the letter of 5th July 2005 on Thames; and that if Total failed to supply Thames with any gas per their agreement, Thames will be entitled to damages and specific performance.

---

[69] *(1917) AC 495.*

28. Can a buyer terminate the contract for excessive delays?

Even though a shipbuilder may extend the date for delivering the vessel if it is affected by force majeure event or excluded delays, the duration of such relief will not be infinite. Under most shipbuilding contracts, a buyer will be able to terminate the contract for excessive delays, of 180 days for either permissible or non-permissible delays, or where the combined aggregate of permissible and non-permissible delays exceed 270 days beyond the contractual delivery date. For an example, see Bimco NBC, Clause 39 (a) (iii), where the buyer can terminate the contract if either permissible or non-permissible delays exceed 180 days; or when both of these delays collectively exceed 270 days. See also, *Adyard Abu Dhabi v SD Marine Services*, (discussed below) where the contract provided that the buyer has the right to cancel the contract for non-permissible delays of 150 days, and where the aggregate permissible and non-permissible delays exceed 180 days.

29. What is the prevention principle?

The essence of the prevention principle is that the promisee cannot insist upon the performance of an obligation which he has prevented the promisor from performing. However, the prevention principle will not apply if the contract provides for an extension of time in respect of the relevant events.

In *Adyard Abu Dhabi v SD Marine Services*[70], Adyard agreed to construct two 50m moorings and special operations support vessels, for SDMS. SDMS rescinded the two shipbuilding contracts as the vessels could not meet their sea trials dates. Adyard relied on the

---

[70] *[2011] EWHC 848 (Comm).*

prevention principle and claimed that SDMS was not entitled to rescind because it was prevented from completing the vessels for sea trials by SDMS' acts. Also, it was entitled to extensions of time for similar reasons, because of the extra work to vary some design items and SDMS's failure to agree (and its refusal to negotiate) on the consequences of the variations.

Mr Justice Hamblen summarized the prevention principle with reference to the judgment of Jackson J in *Multiplex v Honeywell*[71], and said that in a basic shipbuilding contract where a builder had to complete the construction of a vessel and reach certain milestones within a specified time, the builder is entitled to the whole of that period to complete the contract work. However, if the buyer interferes with the work and delays its completion, this is an act of prevention. In such a case, the builder is no longer bound by the strict requirements of the contract as to time. However, while instructions to vary the work may amount to an act of prevention, the prevention principle will not apply if the contract provides for an extension of time for the relevant events. In such a case, completion dates are extended as appropriate and the builder must complete the work by the new date or pay liquidated damages, or accept the contractual consequence of late completion.

The court held that SDMS was entitled to rescind and recover the return of instalments paid with interests for the following reasons:

- The design items were not variations to the contracts; thus, the prevention principle was inapplicable.
- Even if there were any variations, the contract provided for an extension of time for the delay caused.

---

[71] *[2007] Bus LR Digest D109.*

- Even if there were any variations and the contract did not allow for an extension of time, such variations did not cause any delay to the work.
- Even if Adyard were able to prove actual delay, its claim would fail because of non-compliance with the notice provision of the contract.

In the case of *Jiangsu Guoxin Corporation Ltd (Formerly Known as Sainty Marine Corporation Ltd) v Precious Shipping Public Co. Ltd*[72], the shipbuilder agreed to construct 14 bulk carriers for the buyer. The relevant terms of the contract provide that:

- The shipbuilder is entitled to an extension of time (EOT) for delivering the vessel if the delivery of the vessel is delayed by force majeure events or causes beyond the control of the shipbuilder or its sub-contractors. Per Article VIII.1.
- The shipbuilder must notify the buyer of any EOT claim within specified days, failing which the shipbuilder shall not be entitled to an EOT. Per Article VIII.2.
- The buyer could cancel the contract if non-permissible delays exceed 150 days, or the aggregate of permissible and non-permissible delays exceeds 180 days.

After ships 1 and 2 were delivered, the shipbuilder tendered ships 3 to 6, but they were rejected by the buyer. Due to delivery delays, the buyer cancelled the contract for ships 7 and 8. The shipbuilder contended that the unlawful rejection of ships 3 to 6, resulted in the occupation of berths at the yard and the delay to ships 7 and 8. This constituted an act of wrongful prevention on the part of the buyer, and thus, time was set at large[73]. However, the shipbuilder did not give

---

[72] *[2020] EWHC 1030 (Comm).*

[73] *The modern jurisprudence on "time at large" commenced with Lord Denning's judgment in*

notice of the alleged prevention claim. On appeal from arbitration, the court disallowed the shipbuilder's appeal for the following reasons:

- The phrase "or other causes beyond the control of the SELLER or of its Subcontractors" followed by the phrase, 'or by force majeure of any description, whether of the nature indicated by the forgoing or not' indicated two possibilities, and was wide enough to include buyer-induced delays outside the control of the shipbuilder and not due to conventional force majeure events within Article VIII.1. As such, the prevention principle will not apply.
- Regarding notice of delay, the judge said that, even if he was wrong to find that the situation fell within Article VIII.1, the requirement for the shipyard to give notice of force majeure events in Article VIII.2 was wide enough to apply to a prevention claim.
- In cases where foreseeable instances of buyer-induced delay are neither within Article VIII.1 nor another regime, Article VIII.2 should apply to such matters even though they are not within Article VIII.1.
- Subject to limitations, a term is to be implied into the shipbuilding contracts, that neither party should prevent the other from performing its obligations under the contract. However, such implied term and the prevention principle were inapplicable in the present case, as the contract included provisions to extent time.

Trollope & Colls Ltd v North West Metropolitan Regional Hospital Board, which was upheld in the House of Lords. In this case, it was held that: "It is well settled that in building contracts - and in other contracts too - when there is a stipulation for work to be done in a limited time, if one party by his conduct - it may be quite legitimate conduct, such as ordering extra work - renders it impossible or impracticable for the other party to do his work within the stipulated time, then the one whose conduct caused the trouble can no longer insist upon strict adherence to the time stated. He cannot claim any penalties or liquidated damages for non-completion in that time." [1973] 1 W.L.R. 601 at 607.

Delivery of the vessel

30. What are the procedures for delivering the vessel?

Following satisfactory completion of all work, tests, and trials the vessel will be tendered for delivery on the scheduled or extended delivery date, safely afloat alongside a wharf at the shipbuilder's yard and ready in all respects for service, excluding the buyer's preparations such as but not limited to crewing, provisions, and bunkering. Buyer accepts the vessel, by signing a protocol of delivery and acceptance, acknowledging delivery by the shipbuilder and acceptance by the buyer. Where shipbuilder is requested to carry out ant work on the vessel after delivery, it is important to ensure that there is insurance coverage during such work as some builder's risk insurance may have expired upon delivery. Where slot space at the shipyard is limited, the contract will provide that buyer must sail the vessel away within a reasonable timeframe, failing which docking and other charges will be imposed on the buyer. The delivery documents to be provided to the buyer include:

- Protocol of Delivery and Acceptance.
- Builder's Certificate.
- Specified Certificates

- Commercial Invoice.
- Bill of Sale.
- Trials Records.
- Inventory records
- Records of fuels, lubricants, consumable stores, and fresh water.
- Drawings, plans and instruction books.
- Waiver of Liens and Claims.
- Warranty Bond.

Protocol of Delivery and Acceptance (PDA)

A duly signed protocol of delivery and acceptance verifies that vessel have been duly delivered and accepted by buyer on the indicated date. It is also the date when title and risk to the vessel passes from shipbuilder to buyer and signifies the end of builder's risk insurance coverage.

Builder's Certificate

This is the document where the shipbuilder certifies that the vessel was constructed at its shipyard at (address) and delivered to the Buyer (name) on (delivery date). It also includes pertinent technical details about the vessel and is essential for the vessel's registration with relevant flag state authorities, financing, and other purposes.

Commercial Invoice

This provides the details of all the instalments paid and the final installments payable.

Bill of Sale

This substantiates the transfer of ownership or title to the completed vessel from shipbuilder to buyer, and to facilitate the registration of the vessel at relevant Registry of Ships. Also, ship registry, like those in the UK will not recognize the transfer of title to the vessel until the bill of sale is duly registered in their registry. Additionally, the text of the bill of sale will comprise shipbuilder's affirmation that they have the power to transfer the vessel and title to the buyer and that the vessel is free from all encumbrances, debts, maritime liens, mortgages, and any other claims whatsoever.

Trials Records

This comprises the results of the vessel's trials recorded.

Other certificates

This include classification certificates and those required to be provided before or upon delivery of the vessel per the specification. Some contracts may provide that, if, through no fault of the shipbuilder, classification certificates and other certificates are not available at the time of delivery, the buyer shall accept provisional certificates, provided such certificates enable the vessel to be registered and do not impose any restriction on the vessel's trading or operations. In such cases, shipbuilder will have to undertake (with or without security) that formal certificates will be provided to the buyer expeditiously when they are available.

Inventory

This itemizes the vessel's equipment and machinery, including spare gear excluding buyer's supplies.

Records of fuels, lubricants

This comprised a record of the balance of unused fuels, lubricants, consumable stores, and fresh water remaining on board at delivery of the vessel.

Drawings, plans and instruction books

This includes the complete set of drawings, plans, instruction books as stipulated in the specifications.

Waiver of Liens and Claims

This document is where shipbuilder certifies (a) that the vessel is free and clear from all liens, charges and other encumbrances and claims from shipbuilder, its subcontractors and suppliers and any other party claiming through shipbuilder, (b) confirms that all monies due under the shipbuilding contract has been paid in full and that there are no outstanding claims against buyer in respect thereof, and (c) agrees to indemnify buyer against all such liens, charges, encumbrances and claims referred to above.

Warranty Bond

As delivery of the vessel signifies the start of shipbuilder's defects guarantee obligations, this bond is used to secure such obligations. The amount secured is usually subject to negotiation and could be about two per cent of the contract price. Such bond will only be triggered if the shipyard unjustifiably failed or refused to perform its said obligation.

Punch List

This document is prepared during the completion stage of a shipbuilding project listing minor non-conforming work or omission that the shipbuilder must complete prior to delivery of the vessel or within a reasonable time after delivery. In this respect, it should be noted that builder's risks insurance will expire upon delivery of the vessel. Therefore, if shipbuilder is required to carry out any further work on the vessel, reciprocal indemnity and appropriate insurance cover for property damage and personal injury or death for are in place.

31. Will a signed PDA preclude a buyer's claim for damages?

In *Riva Bella SA v Tamsen Yachts GmbH*[74], where the buyer claims damages for alleged deficiencies existing at the date of delivery of a super yacht, the court acknowledges that in certain circumstances, the acceptance of any ship when tendered for delivery by a shipbuilder and the signing of a PDA may preclude a buyer from rejecting the ship (at least with regard to patent defects) and even to preclude a buyer from claiming damages against the seller. However, acceptance will not prevent a claim for damages, save the contract provides that acceptance shall preclude a claim for damages.

In *Saga Cruises BDF Ltd and another v Fincantieri SPA*[75], the owners sued the yard for breach under a docking, repair, and refurbishment agreement. The yard argued that (a) the owners is precluded by the protocol of completion and acceptance, (b) the owners' only remedy is in the defect guarantee provision in clause 12 of the agreement, and (c) such claims are barred under Clause 12. The protocol of completion and acceptance states that: "...The Contractor has today completed the Works and the Owner has accepted that the requirements of the Agreement have been complied with pursuant to the provisions of Clause 9 of the Agreement in all respects except as outlined herein....Each party confirms that, with the exception of the above-described matters ... it has no other requests or claims against the other party whatsoever".

Ms Sara Cockerill QC (sitting as a Deputy High Court Judge) referred to *Gilbert-Ash (Northern) Ltd v Modern Engineering (Bristol) Ltd*[76], where Lord Diplock said that there is a presumption that neither party intends to abandon any remedies for its breach arising by operation of law, and there must be clear express words to rebut this presumption. The judge also, referred to *Stocznia Gdynia SA v*

---

[74] *[2011] EWHC 1434 (Comm).*

[75] *Saga Cruises BDF Ltd and another v Fincantieri SPA [2016] EWHC 1875 (Comm).*

[76] *Lord Diplock in Gilbert-Ash (Northern) Ltd v Modern Engineering (Bristol) Ltd [1974] AC 689.*

Gearbulk Holdings Ltd[77], where Moore-Bick LJ (with whom the other members of the Court agreed) held that: "It is important to remember that any clause in a contract must be construed in the context in which one finds it, both the immediate context of the other terms and the wider context of the transaction as a whole. The court is unlikely to be satisfied that a party to a contract has abandoned valuable rights arising by operation of law unless the terms of the contract make it sufficiently clear that that was intended. The more valuable the right, the clearer the language will need to be." The judge noted the effect of a protocol of delivery in the context of shipbuilding contracts where it is well-established that clear words are needed to displace the right to contractual damages, and held that in the present case, there were no clear words in the protocol of completion and acceptance to displace such right, except to record completion of the work.

In summing, a signed protocol of delivery and acceptance, indicating acceptance of a vessel will not prevent a claim for damages[78], save where the contract expressly provides that acceptance shall preclude a claim for damages or where the parties expressly agree to vary the terms of the contract or to give up any claim for damages or where there is some kind of estoppel, as in *Olympic Airlines SA (in special liquidation) v ACG Acquisition XX LLC*[79].

32. When can a buyer refuse to take delivery of the vessel?

The buyer is obligated to take delivery of the vessel when the same is in a delivery state, and under SOGA s61(5), the vessel will be in a deliverable when they are in such a state that the buyer would under the contract be bound to take delivery of them. In *McDougall v Aeromarine of Emsworth Ltd*[80], Lord Diplock (then Diplock J) said

---

[77] *Stocznia Gdynia SA v Gearbulk Holdings Ltd [2009] EWCA Civ 75, [2010] QB 27.*
[78] *Saga Cruises BDF Ltd and another v Fincantieri SPA [2016] EWHC 1875 (Comm)..*
[79] *[2012] EWHC 1070 (Comm), [2013] EWCA Civ 369.*
[80] *McDougall v Aeromarine of Emsworth Ltd [1958] 1 WLR 1126 (QB).*

that the buyer can refuse delivery if he is not reasonably satisfied with the performance of vessel at the conclusion of the acceptance trials. He construed the expression "performance" widely to include the standard of workmanship and materials and the compliance of the vessel with the specification, as a narrow interpretation would mean the seller had fulfilled his contractual obligation even though the interior fittings were incomplete or different from those specified so long as the vessel sailed well. He went on to say that: "...because when the vessel is first tendered by the seller for acceptance trials the buyer is reasonably dissatisfied with her, he is entitled to treat the defects then existing as a breach of condition, ...The buyer is entitled to refuse to accept delivery of the vessel in its existing state, but, if the defect is one that can be remedied, and remedied within a time which will still enable the seller to deliver within the period of delivery permitted by the contract, the buyer is not, in my view, entitled to treat the contract as repudiated by the seller by reason of the existence of such defects at the time when the vessel is first tendered for acceptance".

Thus, if the non-conformity is minor, and could be remedied before the contractual drop-dead date[81], a buyer cannot lawfully terminate the contract. Also, some contracts may provide that for minor defects, the buyer will accept the vessel provided shipbuilder undertake to remedy such defects within a reasonable time, and comply with certain stipulated conditions, which may include providing security.

---

[81]*Drop-dead date: The last date an event must take place, failing which the contract may be lawfully terminated. In shipbuilding contract, this will usually mean the day after force majeure delays exceed an aggregate of 180 or specified days, or the aggregate of permissible and non-permissible delays exceed 270 or specified days.*

Defects Warranty

33. What are the essential elements of a warranty clause?

Under standard industry practice, the shipbuilder will be required to guarantee that the vessel, its materials, equipment, and machinery (excluding buyer supplies, save for its proper installation) shall be newly manufactured, and be free of defects in design, material, and workmanship. The terms of the warranty clause will comprise the guaranteed duration, scope, coverage, notice procedure, claim verification, repair location, disclaimers, and limitations.

The Guaranteed Duration

This will typically be 12 months from the delivery of the vessel. Such duration may be extended for another 12 months for repaired or replaced items, starting from the repairs or replacement date, and cap at 18 months from the vessel delivery date. Paint guarantee will typically be about five (5) years, with allowance for depreciation.

Coverage

This will include the repair or replacement of defective design, workmanship, materials, equipment, and machinery, excluding buyer supplies, save for its installation. The shipbuilder will be responsible for the costs and expenses of repair or replacement and disposal of faulty item, re-delivery of repaired items, insurance, packing, handling, personnel's travel expenses (excluding transport to any offshore site), lodging, labour, and material cost. The contract may also provide that shipbuilder shall not be liable for the costs or charges in connection with mooring, dry-docking, vessel's fuels, assisting vessels, towing of any vessel, docking of any vessel, divers, third party tools, wages (other than the wages of the shipbuilder's employees), board and lodging offshore, transport to and from any offshore location, and heavy lift operations. Where it relates to the vessel's performance, this is addressed under a distinct clause which deals with the allowable margin for excess or deficiency related to speed, fuel consumption, deadweight deficiency, and cubic capacity. If such allowable margin is exceeded or otherwise during pre-delivery tests and trials, the shipbuilder may be subject to liquidated damages and in the worst-case scenario rejection of the vessel.

See examples in industry standard form shipbuilding contracts:

- AWES Article 5, (a) Speed, (b) Deadweight Capacity, (c) Grain/bale Capacity, (d) Fuel Consumption.
- Bimco NBC, Clauses 8, Speed Deficiency, 9. Excessive Fuel Consumption, 10. Deadweight Deficiency, and 11. Cubic Capacity Deficiency respectively.
- NSF, Article IV, 2 Speed Deficiency, 3. Deficiency in Fuel Consumption, 4. Deficiency in Deadweight, 5. Deficiency in Cubic Capacity.
- SAJ, Article III, 2. Speed, 3. Fuel Consumption, 4 Deadweight.

Notice Procedure

Depending on the language, the notice requirement will usually be a condition precedent, requiring the buyer to give notice of any defects to shipbuilder within a specified period. The rationale for this is to have the defects verified and rectified as soon as possible to prevent deterioration or further damage.

Claim Verification

For the purpose of ensuring that the claim is within the warranty clause, some contracts will provide that upon receipt of any guarantee claim, the shipbuilder shall respond timely, inspect, and verify the validity of the claim before any repair or replacement is carried out. To expedite resolution of disputes concerning this, parties may agree that if the shipbuilder rejects the warranty claim, and this is disputed by the buyer, who nevertheless requests shipbuilder to carry out repairs or replacement, the buyer shall pay for the work upon the shipbuilder's undertaking to refund to the buyer within 14 days such sums as may subsequently be negotiated or awarded at mediation or arbitration.

Repair at Third-Party Shipyard

Where it is impractical to bring the vessel to the shipbuilder's yard, the parties may agree that repair or replacement will be carried out at a third-party shipyard. In such an event, the contract may provide for the shipbuilder, to supply replacement parts or materials to the vessel at its own expense. To prevent exorbitant rates at such third-party shipyard, it may be agreed that the rates for repairs or replacements (other than those supplied by the shipbuilder) carried out by the buyer at such third-party shipyard shall be at such third-party shipyard's rate or the shipbuilder's published rate, whichever is lower.

Limitations and Disclaimers

The warranty clause will commonly include limitations and disclaimers that it will not apply to defects claim not notified within the specified time limit and to defects due to or caused by the following:

- Normal wear and tear.
- Perils of the sea or navigation, overloading or due to corrosion, accidents, fire, improper loading, or stowage.
- Negligent, omission or improper use and failure to maintain the vessel by the buyer or firm operating the vessel on buyer's behalf.
- Repairs by buyer or any third party other than shipbuilder or its authorized representative.

In addition to the above, other limitations or disclaimers will include provisions that the guarantee shall be in lieu of all other guarantee, warranty and/or condition (except of title), express, implied or statutory and all liabilities at common law or in contract, tort or otherwise, including without limitation, consequential or indirect loss as defined in the contract or by reason of the defects or by reason of repairs or other work done to the vessel to remedy such defects, strict liability and negligence, whether caused by acts or omissions of the shipbuilder's sole or concurrent negligence.

Indemnity

To manage risks of loss or damage during the repair or replacement, prudent shipbuilder may require that whenever any repair or replacement work is carried out on board the vessel at any location, the parties shall indemnify each other, regardless of fault for (a) damage to their own property (and those of their own employees and subcontractors) and (b) personal injuries, disease, or death of their own employees and those of their subcontractors.

34. Must notice of defects claim be given timely?

Shipbuilder's defects guarantee obligation is not absolute and the buyer will usually be required to give notice of defects to shipbuilder within a specified period, usually within 5 working days of discovery of any defects, (and at any rate within the contractual guarantee period) failing which any purported defects claim may be rejected or time-barred. In the case of *Neon Shipping Inc v Foreign Economic 7 Technical Corporation*[82], the parties entered into a shipbuilding contract for the design, build and supply of a bulk carrier governed by English law. Three years after delivery of the vessel, buyer claimed that that the cargo cranes were faulty. No notice of the defects about the cranes was given within the guarantee period of 12 months. The shipbuilder denied liability in respect of the alleged defects, and further relied upon Article XI of the Contract which provides under:

- Article XI: that shipbuilder guarantees that the vessel, and all parts manufactured or supplied by shipbuilder will be seaworthy and contractual in all respects and will be free from all defects ("Guarantee Defects"), for 12 months from the date of delivery ("Guarantee Period"). *[paraphrased]*
- Article XI.2: that buyer must notify shipbuilder promptly after discovery of any Guarantee defects, and shipbuilder shall not be liable for a Guarantee Defect unless notice of such defect is sent to shipbuilder within 30 calendar days after the end of the Guarantee Period. *[paraphrased]*

Further, the contract provides that the guarantee is limited to the guarantee period and buyer waives all other remedies, warranties, guarantees or liabilities, express or implied, arising by law or otherwise, including without limitation any obligation of shipbuilder as to fitness, merchantability, and consequential damages, regardless of shipbuilder's negligence. The arbitrators concluded that implied

---

[82] *Neon Shipping Inc v Foreign Economic 7 Technical Corporation Co. of China and others [2016] EWHC 399 (Comm).*

term as to fitness for purpose was excluded and the 12-month time-bar provision excluded all claims not so notified. On appeal, the buyer submitted that Article XI.1 comprises two separate guarantees or Part 1 and Part 2 claims.

- Part 1 claim was that the vessel was not "seaworthy and contractual" within Article XI.1, and a failure or inadequacy in the cranes supplied by third-party suppliers, leading to inadequate performance and unfitness for purpose. The Buyer argued that the comma after "in all respects" signifies the end of the reference to Part 1 claims. They argued that "and" after the comma is disjunctive.
- Part 2 was that the vessel was not "free from all defects which are due to defective design, construction, calculation, material or workmanship", which requires notification to be made within the notice period of 30 days after the end of the Guarantee Period.
- In addition, the buyer also argued that the notice provisions in Article XI.2 was not applicable as their claim was in respect of Part 1 claim.

The appeal court upheld the arbitrators' decision that the 12-month time-bar provision in Article XI of the contract applies to any and all claims whatsoever and dismissed the buyer's appeal. They view the division or bifurcation of Article XI.1 as wholly artificial as there was no real dichotomy between two different claims. Also, there was no commercial or other justification for two different claims. They added that "the argument is constructed as a tabula in naufragio *[a plank in a shipwreck]* for a Buyer who has not given notice."

35. Are shipbuilders liable for post-warranty defects?

In *China Shipbuilding Corporation v Nippon Yusen Kabukishi Kaisha Galaxy Shipping Pte Ltd.*[83], the court had to consider the effect of time limit for notification and rectification of guarantee defects in three bulk carrier construction contracts. The vessels were guarantee against defect in materials and workmanship for 12 months following buyer's acceptance of the vessels. Also, the shipbuilder was not liable for any defects discovered after the said 12-month period and for any defects in the vessel other than the defects specified in the contracts.

After the expiry of the guarantee period, defects in the erection welding of the vessels were discovered in two of the vessels and each suffered a casualty involving an ingress of water through the shell plating. The buyers contented inter alia, that the shipbuilder's liability for defective welding were not excluded as such defects were a breach of expressed terms in the contract which requires the shipbuilder to construct the vessel in accordance with the contract and specification; in a sound and workmanlike manner; according to first class shipbuilding practice, and supply materials that complies with classification society's requirements. The buyers claimed damages for the cost of repairing the welding of the first two of the vessels and for the depreciated value of all the vessels.

The arbitrators decided in favour of the buyers. On appeal, Mr. Justice Thomas held inter alia, that the defect guarantee clause must be read as a whole, because it provided a comprehensive code for the guarantee defects against all defects in material and workmanship for a period of 12 months following acceptance of the vessel. Thus, the shipbuilder was not liable for any defects discovered after the said 12-month period and for any defects in the vessel other than the defects specified in the contracts.

---

83 *[2000] EWHC 211 (Comm).*

36. What are the limits of a shipbuilder's warranty obligations?

While most shipbuilder's warranty obligations are limited to the those specified in the contract; notably with exclusion of statutory implied terms and consequential loss, buyers may sometimes try to claim for damages and losses beyond what was stipulated in the contract. In *Star Polaris LLC v HHIC-PHIL INC.*[84], the contract comprised a twelve (12) month guarantee period for defective materials, design errors, construction miscalculation and/or poor workmanship, provided such defects are not caused by inter alia, perils of the seas, normal wear and tear or mismanagement of the vessel and other clauses as stipulated in the Article IX.1. The positive obligations of the shipbuilder were to remedy any defects under the guarantee by carrying out all necessary repairs or replacements at the shipyard, if reasonably practical or elsewhere. [Article IX 3]. Article IX.4(a) provides that shipbuilder shall have no liability above and beyond its express guarantee obligations. Some months after delivery, the vessel suffered serious engine failure and was towed to the shipbuilder's yard for repairs. The buyer started arbitration proceedings against the shipyard claiming the cost of repairs to the vessel, towage fees, agency fees, survey fees, off-hire and off-hire bunkers, and diminution in value of the vessel.

The arbitration tribunal found that the shipyard was in breach of its warranty of quality because of weld spatters in the pipework at delivery. Hence, the buyer could recover the cost of repairs to the vessel. However, the shipyard's responsibility under Article IX was limited to the repair of defects listed in the said Article. Also, as the buyer's claim for associated financial costs caused by the ship's engine failure and diminution in the vessel's value were "consequential or special losses, damages or expenses" in its cause-

---

[84] *[2016] EWHC 2941 (Comm).*

and-effect sense, they were expressly excluded by Article IX (4) (a) the contract.

On appeal, the buyer argued that the words "consequential or special losses" should be construed per the second limb of the rule in Hadley v Baxendale. Also, as the said words "consequential" were paired with the word "special losses," this indicates the parties' intention that such losses should fall under the second limb losses of the rule in Hadley v. Baxendale. In dismissing the buyer's appeal, the court held that:

- Consequential or special losses, damages or expenses does not mean losses, damages, or expenses within the second limb of Hadley v Baxendale but does have the wider meaning of financial losses caused by guaranteed defects, over and beyond the cost of replacement and repair of physical damage.
- The notice provision requiring buyer to give "full particulars of the defect and the extent of the damage, but excluding consequential damage, illustrates that there is a distinction between physical defects and damage on the one hand and consequential damage on the other. [Article IX.2]
- The positive obligations of the shipbuilder were to remedy any defects by making all necessary repairs or replacements at the shipyard, if reasonably practical or elsewhere. [Article IX 3].
- Article IX.4(a) clearly provides that there is no liability above and beyond the express obligations undertaken by the shipbuilder.
- Therefore, financial losses consequent upon physical damage are not covered by the guarantee.
- Also, there is no express provision which gives rise to a claim for financial loss, lost profit, or diminution of value.

The vessel and classification

37. What are the details in the description of the vessel clause?

This will include the shipbuilder's duty to design, construct, equip and deliver the vessel per the contract and specification; and the requirements of classification society and regulatory bodies.[85] The principal dimensions and particulars the vessel will be summarized, (see below) with reference to its full details in the specification.

Length Overall
Length between Perpendiculars (approximate)
Breadth Moulded (approximate)
Depth to Main Deck from Base Line
Scantling Draught, Moulded
Draught at Assigned Load line
Bollard Pull (approximate)
Trial Speed (approximate)
Main Electrical
Propulsion Plant
Make: Type and Number
Electrical Power (At MCR)

---

[85] *AWES, Article 1 - Subject of Contract, Bimco Newbuilding, Section 1, Vessel NSF, Article II - The Vessel. Description and Class, and SAJ, Article 1 - Description and class.*

The word "approximate" above may indicate the allowable tolerance margin under shipbuilding industry practice. It will be a question of fact when issues do arise. The shipbuilder will provide the hull number to identify the vessel under construction. On the question of whether such hull number could be construed as a contractual description and thus a condition; see the case of *Reardon Smith Line Ltd v Yngvar Hansen-Tangen (the Diana Prosperity*[86], below.

38. Are classification societies liable for negligence?

A topic that has been the source of much debate is whether the classification society is liable for negligence in the conduct of its services. In *Mariola Marine Corporation v Lloyd's Register of Shipping*[87], the buyer bought a vessel which was found to be defective and unseaworthy. Lloyd's Register had retained the vessel in class after a survey. The buyer sued Lloyd's Register for loss suffered, alleging that they had relied on class certificate issued by Lloyd's Register. The court held that there was no relationship of proximity sufficient to conclude that a duty of care in negligence existed between Lloyd's Register and the buyer.

In *Marc Rich & Co AG and Others v Bishop Rock Marine Co and Others (The Nicholas H)*[88], after a crack was discovered in the vessel's hull, classification society Nippon Kaiji Kyokai ("NKK.") was engaged to conduct survey and provide recommendations. The NKK's surveyor initially recommended permanent repairs, but the ship owners were reluctant as it would involve dry docking the vessel, discharge and reloading of the cargo. The surveyor then decided that the vessel could proceed to the discharge port after temporary repairs.

---

[86] *1976] 1 WLR 989 HL.*
[87] *[1990] 1 Lloyd's Rep 54.*
[88] *[1995] UKHL 4, [1996] 1 AC 211.*

However, during the voyage the temporary repairs cracked, and the vessel sank, leading to a total loss of vessel and cargo. The value of the cargo was over US$6 million. The cargo owners settled their claim with the shipowner for US$500,000 and went after NKK for US$5.7 million. The issue before the court was whether NKK owed a duty of care to the cargo owners (a third party), for the damage caused to the cargo arising from its surveyor's negligence. In order to prevail the cargo owners had to prove foreseeability, proximity and that it is fair, just, and reasonable to impose such a duty on NKK. The judge of first instance found in favor of the cargo owners, but this was overruled by the CoA. The cargo owners' appeal to the House of Lords was dismissed. After noting that in England no classification society, engaged by owners to perform a survey, has ever been held liable to cargo owners on the ground of a careless conduct of any survey, Lord Steyn (for the majority) held[89], that the recognition of a duty would be unfair, unjust, and unreasonable to NKK due to the following factors below.

- It was the shipowner's duty to ensure that the vessel was seaworthy, and the NKK surveyor's carelessness did not involve direct infliction of physical damage.
- There was no contact between the cargo owners and NKK, and the former were not aware that NKK was brought in to survey the vessel.
- The dealings between shipowners and cargo owners are based on a contractual structure, the Hague Rules, and tonnage limitation, on which the insurance of international trade depends. Under the insurance system, the potential liability of shipowners to cargo owners is limited under the Hague Rules and by virtue of tonnage limitation provisions.

---

[89] *On the assumption that there was a sufficient degree of proximity in this case to fulfil that requirement for the existence of a duty of care.*

- If classification societies are liable to cargo owners, this will enable cargo owners, or their insurers, to disturb the balance created by the Hague Rules and Hague-Visby Rules as well as by tonnage limitation provisions. Thus, enabling cargo owners to recover in tort against a peripheral party to the prejudice of the protection of shipowners under the existing system.
- The potential exposure of classification societies to claims by cargo owners will be large; and classification societies will have to pay extra cost to obtain appropriate liability risks insurance, and as classification societies will require owners to give appropriate indemnities, shipowners will ultimately have to pay.
- Classification societies are independent non-profit-making entity promoting the collective welfare, namely the safety of lives and ships at sea. If they become the ready alternative target of cargo owners, who already have contractual claims against shipowners, they might adopt, to the detriment of their traditional role, a more defensive position. They might be unwilling to survey vessels which most urgently require independent examination.
- Also, if a duty is recognized in this case there is no reason why it should not extend to annual surveys, docking surveys, intermediate surveys, special surveys, boiler surveys, and so forth.
- The system of settling cargo claims against shipowners is a relatively simple one and such claims are settled between the two sets of insurers. If a duty is held to exist in this case as between NKK and cargo owners, classification societies would become potential defendants in many cases and the settlement process would inevitably become more complicated and expensive.

Quality and implied terms

39. When may a vessel's quality standard be upheld?

This will depend on the contract terms and whether statutory implied terms are applicable. If a contract stipulates that the quality standard of the vessel must be in accordance with "first class" shipbuilding standard and practice, this may indicate a higher standard than ordinarily reasonable skill and care. In the case of *Rolls-Royce Power Engineering Plc, Allen Power Engineering Limited v Ricardo Consulting Engineers*[90], it was said that:

> "… an obligation to provide services of first-class quality does conceptually, and may in practice, involve an obligation going beyond a requirement merely to use reasonable skill and care in providing the services."

40. Can implied terms under SOGA be excluded?

Implied terms under the SOGA may be expressly excluded, and in such a case, the shipbuilder is only obligated to construct a vessel that conforms to the contract and specification. However, if implied terms are not expressly excluded, implied terms under the SOGA[91]

---

90 *[2003] EWHC 2871 (TCC).*
91 *Sale of Goods Act 1979 (as amended by SSGA 1994).*

will apply to the contract, and the vessel must correspond with description, be of satisfactory quality, and fit for purpose.

Under s13(1) SOGA, where there is a contract for the sale of goods by description, there is an implied term that the goods will correspond with the description. Previously, where goods do not correspond with description, this has been construed against the shipbuilder strictly. More recently, the House of Lords held that it was only where a particular item in a description constituted a substantial ingredient of the identity of the thing sold that it was to be treated as a condition.

In *Reardon Smith Line Ltd v Yngvar Hansen-Tangen*[92] *(the Diana Prosperity)*, Reardon Smith entered into a long-term time charter of a tanker. The tanker was to be built by Osaka Shipbuilding Ltd and described as Yard No. 354 at Osaka Zosen. However, as Osaka's yard was too small to construct the tanker, Osaka subcontracted the construction of the vessel to another yard, Oshima and identified as hull 004. The completed tanker complied with specification but as the oil market had fallen sharply, the charterers rejected the vessel. The buyers contended that the vessel did not correspond with the contractual description in that it was Oshima 004 and not Osaka 354.

The House of Lords held that the hull number of the vessel had no special significance to raise it to a matter of fundamental obligation. The vessel contracted for was the vessel tendered. The hull number was not intended to be part of the description of the vessel and in the context of the contract was without a significant meaning, other than to identify the vessel which had not been constructed nor did it have a name at the time of fixing the charter. It was only where

---

[92] *[1976] 1 WLR 989 HL.*

a particular item in a description constituted a substantial ingredient of the identity of the thing sold that it was to be treated as a condition.

Under s14(2) SOGA, where the seller sells goods in the course of a business, there is an implied term that the goods supplied under the contract are of satisfactory quality. The core requirement as to quality is that the goods supplied should be of 'satisfactory quality'. Goods are of satisfactory quality if they meet the standard that a reasonable person would regard as satisfactory, taking into account, the description of the goods, the price (if relevant) and all the other relevant circumstances. The standard is thus one of reasonable expectations. This is amplified by subsection 14(2B) SOGA, which lists several factors to be taken into account as 'aspects of quality' in an appropriate case. They include (a) fitness for all the purposes for which goods of that kind are commonly supplied, (b) appearance and finish, (c) freedom from minor defects, (d) safety, and (e) durability.

In *Clegg and another v Olle Andersson*[93], The buyer rejected a yacht with overweight keel. The court of appeal held that a reasonable person would consider that the yacht was not of satisfactory quality because of the overweight keel, the adverse effect it had on safety and the need for more than minimal remedial work. The buyer had therefore established a breach of condition under s 14(2) SOGA1979.

In *Dalmare SpA v Union Maritime Ltd & Valor Shipping Ltd*[94], the shipbuilder agreed to sell a vessel to the buyers, under a Memorandum of Agreement ("the MOA"), based on the Norwegian Saleform 1993 ("Saleform 93"). Clause 11 of the MOA provides that:

- The vessel shall be delivered and taken over as she was at the time of inspection, fair wear and tear excepted, with her class maintained and extended to 30 September 2009 without condition

93 *[2003] 1 All ER (Comm) 721.*
94 *[2012] EWHC 3537.*

and recommendation, free of average damage affecting the vessel's class.

- The vessel's continuous survey cycles of machinery are to be as per current machinery continuous status.
- Her international, national, class and trading certificates clean, should be valid until 30 September 2009, except ISSC and SMC to be valid at time of delivery only.

The buyers inspected the vessel and carried out an underwater survey, which revealed no bottom damage affecting its class. Their agents also inspected the class records but failed to pick up a reference in the class records referring to damage to the No.1 crankpin of the main engine. A month after delivery, as the vessel departed to load a cargo of diesel, the main engine broke down due to failure of No.1 crankpin bearing. The buyers contended that the shipbuilders were in breach of the MOA either because the ovality was "average damage affecting class" within clause 11 (which the tribunal rejected) or a breach as to satisfactory quality implied into the MOA by virtue of section 14(2) of the Sale of Goods Act 1979 ("SOGA").

The Tribunal held that the implied term as to satisfactory quality was to be implied into the MOA. On appeal, the court concluded that the first sentence of clause 11 of the MOA did not exclude implied term as to satisfactory quality and that the shipbuilders were in breach of that implied term.

The court also agree with buyers' counsel that implied terms under section 14 SOGA will apply to English law contract of sale as to any other, unless the parties (a) have contracted out of section 14 SOGA, by either expressly contracting out as in the case of the detailed clause considered by Cooke J in *Air Transworld Ltd v Bombardier Inc*[95]; or (b) by a clear and unequivocal statement of an

---

[95] *[2012] EWHC 243 (Comm); [2012] 1 Lloyd's Rep 349).*

alternative regime as to quality which was wholly inconsistent with section 14(2) implied term as to satisfactory quality, such as an entire agreement clause.

Under s14(3) SOGA, where the seller sells goods in the course of a business and the buyer, expressly or by implication, makes known to the seller, any particular purpose for which the goods are being bought, there is an implied term that the goods supplied under the contract are reasonably fit for that purpose, whether or not that is purpose for which such goods are commonly supplied, except where the circumstances show that the buyer did not rely, or that it is unreasonable for him to rely, on the skill or judgment of the seller.

In *Cammell Laird & Co v Manganese Bronze & Brass Co*[96], the buyer provided the shipbuilder with a specification which stated that the leading edges of the propellers were not accurately shown in the drawings and that it was for the shipbuilder to use their own judgment as to how to taper the propeller fines lines. The ship failed a performance test because the propellers created too much noise. The court held that it was sufficient if reliance was placed on the skill and judgment of the shipbuilder to some substantial extent. Regarding the part of the work that was left to the skill and judgment of the shipbuilder, there was a breach of implied condition that the propeller should be reasonably fit for the purpose in which it was required. However, if the shipbuilder were neither aware nor were in a position to exercise skill and judgment, the position will be different.

In *Slater v Finning*[97], new camshaft was fitted to a fishing vessel, the 'Aquarius II'. The first new camshaft and subsequent two replacements failed. The owner eventually sold the vessel, and the engine was replaced. The old engine (with no replacement to the camshaft) was fitted into another vessel, and it worked satisfactorily for long periods. The House of Lords held that the 'Aquarius II' had

---

[96] *(1934) AC 402.*

[97] *[1996] 2 Lloyd's Rep 353.*

an unknown and unusual characteristic, a tendency to create excessive torsional resonance noise. The camshaft was required to be fitted in the engine of a vessel with particular abnormality or idiosyncrasy. As the defendants were neither aware nor in a position to exercise skill and judgment, they were not liable.

In *Neon Shipping v Foreign Economic 7 Technical Corporation Co. of China and another*[98], concerning a warranty claim which was ultimately decided by the court to be time-barred, the court also had to consider whether (1) s.14(3) of the Sale of Goods Act 1979 ("SOGA") is inapplicable to a shipbuilding project in which the vessel is built for use in standardized trades, or s.14(3) applies in any case where goods have been ordered for their normal purpose, and (2) whether, for the purposes of s55(2) SOGA[99], a clause containing a general description of the goods to be sold can be regarded as inconsistent with the implied terms provided in s.14 SOGA? Regarding the first question, the court stated obiter dicta, that for the purpose of s.14 (3), there is no need for there to be a particular purpose identified, and normal use in accordance with the contractual specification will suffice. Concerning the second question, the court's answer was: "It depends."

41. When is a breach of implied terms a breach of warranty?

Section 15A, SOGA (as amended by SSGA 1994), provides that if the seller's breach of a term implied by ss13, 14 or 15 is so slight that it would be unreasonable for the buyer to reject the goods, then the breach is to be treated as a breach of warranty. The test is an objective one, from the point of view of a reasonable buyer. The burden of proof is on the seller to show that the breach is so slight that

---

98 *[2016] EWHC 399 (Comm)*

99 *Under Section 55(2) SOGA, an express condition or warranty does not negative a condition or warranty implied by this Act unless inconsistent with it.*

it would be unreasonable for the buyer to reject the goods. Under the Act, a breach of condition will entitle the party not at fault to treat the contract as repudiated whereas a breach of warranty only gives rise to a right to damages, but not a right to reject the goods and treat the contract as repudiated.

Financial terms

42. What are the components of the contract price?

This will basically be derived from the price estimates, which include the pricing of the following items.

General expenses	Navigation and communications
Hull & superstructure	Launching & certification fees
Hull preparation	Documentation fees
Outfitting	Insurance
Painting	Designer's fees
Piping system	Guarantee & bonds
Propulsion and auxiliary	Financing costs
Electrical and electronic	Marketing costs
Fire fighting	Legal costs
Safety equipment	Commission
Accommodation	Office facilities
Carpentry	Warranty expenses
Air-conditioning	Overheads and profit

The contract price will usually be a fixed lump sum, in specified currency, and payable per milestone pre-delivery instalments. The contract price will be subject to adjustment for variation, liquidated damages for delays, vessel's performance deficiency or excess. Some contracts may provide that the contract price will not be subject to any set-off or retention by the buyer under any circumstances, save where duly authorized under the liquidated damages clause.

Unless, expressly agreed, the contract price will not be adjusted for currency fluctuation or any increase in the price of materials, and any attempt by a shipbuilder to increase the price unilaterally may be dismissed for lack of consideration or economic duress or fraud, except in special circumstances where the buyer benefited.

43. When will a demand for extra payments be wrongful?

Unless extra or additional sums are permitted under a variation order, any attempt by shipbuilder to wrongfully exerts undue pressure on buyer to pay additional sums may amount to economic duress, rendering such agreement voidable.

In *North Ocean Shipping v Hyundai Construction Ltd (The Atlantic Baron),*[100] *Hyundai* (the shipbuilder) agreed to build a tanker for North Ocean (the shipowner). The price for the vessel was payable by 5 instalments. The price was not to be adjusted except in certain events. Hyundai had to provide a letter of credit as security for repayment of instalments in the event of performance default.

After the first instalment had been paid, the US dollar was devalued by 10%. Hyundai requested an extra 10% price increase for the remaining four instalments. North Ocean rejected this. However, as they have a charter for the tanker, North Ocean proposed that the

---

[100] *[1979] QB 705.*

matter be referred for arbitration. Hyundai rejected this proposal and demanded that North Ocean provide a decisive reply on the 10% price increase, failing which they will terminate the contract.

Pursuant to an Agreement on 28/29 June 1973, North Ocean agreed to the 10% price increase and in turn requested Hyundai to increase the letter of credit amount correspondingly with the price increase. Hyundai accepted this and North Ocean paid the remaining four instalments with an additional 10% on each instalment without protest. Hyundai also increased their letter of credit for repayment of instalments. North Ocean accepted delivery of the vessel without protest and later claim for the return of the additional sums paid.

Judge Mocatta held that although the rule[101] that a promise by one party to a contract to fulfil his existing contractual duty toward the other party did not constitute good consideration, there was consideration as Hyundai had increased the amount in the letter of credit. But the agreement was obtained under economic duress and voidable. However, by failing to protest, along with the delay in initiating their claim, North Ocean had affirmed the agreement, and was bound by it. Thus, North Ocean could not recover the extra 10% price increase on the four instalments which they have paid.

44. Is there any implied duty of co-operation in shipbuilding contracts?

Where the contract stipulates that all invoices submitted for progressive payment must be accompanied by a signed document verifying that the relevant milestone has been achieved, disputes may arise when the buyer unreasonably refused to countersign such

[101] *Stilk v Myrick (1809) 170 ER 1168, 2 Camp 317.*

document, thereby delaying payment. A sample of a shipbuilding progressive instalment payment terms is illustrated below.

Milestones	Percentage of Contract Price
Within 5 banking days of contract signing	
Upon placing the order for steel	
Upon the start of steel cutting	
Upon keel laying (first block erected)	
Upon fabricating 50% of the steel hull	
Upon fabricating 100% of the steel hull	
Upon erecting 50% of the steel hull	
Upon erecting 100% of the steel hull	
Upon Launching	
Upon Delivery	

In *Swallowfalls Ltd v Monaco Yachting & Technologies S.A.M. & Anr* [102], Swallowfalls commissioned the yacht from Monaco Yachting & Technologies S.A.M. ("MYT"). The actual construction work was to be carried out at La Spezia in Italy by Cantiere San Marco SRL ("the Yard"). Under the Construction Agreement the price of the yacht was payable by 11 instalments when MYT had achieved what is known as "milestones", with a final 10% for the 11th milestone payable on delivery.

Subsequently, MYT had difficulty in meeting their obligations under the subcontract with the Yard, and Swallowfalls provided a series of loans to MYT. After MYT repeatedly failed to repay the loans, Swallowfalls declared MYT in material breach and demanded payment of the balance of the loan. MYT refuted Swallowfalls' claim

---

[102] *[2014] EWCA Civ 186.*

and asserted, amongst other things, that Swallowfalls failed to countersign stage certificates for the milestone achieved so as to enable the loan to be repaid by MYT. MYT contended inter alia, that a term should be implied that: "... Swallowfalls would cooperate with MYT in the confirmation of the achievement of Milestones and, in particular, the countersignature of stage certificates."

The CoA unanimously held that the Swallowfalls has an implied obligation to co-operate and sign the stage certificate if the relevant milestone has been reached.

Guarantees in shipbuilding

45. What are refund and payment guarantee?

The propose of refund and payment guarantees[103] in shipbuilding contracts is to manage counter-party risks. As such, most buyers will require a refund guarantee from the shipbuilder for the repayment of installments in the event that the buyer terminate the contract lawfully. Likewise, shipbuilders may require a payment guarantee from the buyer to secure buyer's payment obligation. This is often required if one or more of the following concerns are present: (a) the payment terms are heavily back loaded; (b) buyer is special purpose one-ship company with limited assets, and (c) buyer is from a jurisdiction where the enforcement of any arbitration award or court judgement may be difficult. Depending on its language as a whole, interpreted in its particular commercial context, such guarantees may be a traditional guarantee or demand guarantee; with different legal implications. A guarantor's liability under a traditional guarantee is secondary and dependent upon the liability of the principal debtor. It is also referred to as "see to it" guarantees, where the guarantor's obligation is "to see to it" that the debtor

---

[103] *Such guarantees may be issued by banks, financial institutions, insurers and at times, the parent company of the parties.*

performed its own obligation to the creditor. In contrast, a demand guarantee can simply be activated by a demand made on the guarantor, and is payable without proof or condition, and independent of the underlying shipbuilding contract.

In *Gold Coast v Caja De Ahorros Del*[104] the issue was whether the bank refund guarantee was payable on demand or after the shipbuilder's liability has been determined by arbitration. Under the guarantee the bank had to pay specified amounts on first written demand, subject to receipt of a certificate issued by Lloyd's Bank, stating the instalment amount paid to shipbuilder; the date of such payment; and that buyer have become entitled to a refund pursuant to the contract and that the shipbuilder has not made such refund. The CoA held that the instrument was a first demand guarantee as the bank has assumed "irrevocable and unconditional undertaking", obligation, that the bank "will pay" on a first written demand. Also, the condition of payment only requires a certificate, with no reference to arbitration or any underlying liability under the shipbuilding contract. The instrument also contains its own dispute resolution provisions.

In *Wuhan Guoyu Logistics Group Co Ltd and Another v Emporiki Bank of Greece SA*[105], the payment guarantee provide for payment to be made on the shipbuilder's first written demand, stating that the buyer is in default its payment obligation for 20 days. Payment is to be made "immediately" without any request being made to the shipbuilder to take any action against the buyer. Also, the guarantee provided that the bank's obligations shall not be affected or prejudiced by any dispute between the shipbuilder and the buyer under the shipbuilding contract or by any delay by the shipbuilder in the construction or delivery of the vessel. The CoA found for the

---

[104] *Gold Coast Ltd v Caja De Ahorros Del Mediterraneo & Others (2001) EWCA Civ 1806.*
[105] *[2012] EWCA Civ 1629.*

shipbuilder on the basis that while the interpretation of a guarantee is dependent on the words used, there is a presumption that, if certain elements are present in the document, the document will be construed in one way or the other. Such elements were propounded in Paget's Law of Banking 11th edition under "Contract of Suretyship v. demand guarantee", which provide that where an instrument:

"(i) Relates to an underlying transaction between the parties in different jurisdictions (ii) Is issued by a bank (iii) Contains an undertaking to pay "on demand" (with or without the words "first" and/or "written") (iv) Does not contain clauses excluding or limiting the defences available to a guarantor, it will almost always be construed as a demand guarantee." According to the appellate court, the words "will almost always be" amount to a presumption which was by then fully justified by the Court of Appeal authorities[106], ..."

Such presumption was subsequently approved by the CoA in *Gold Coast Ltd v Caja de Ahorros*[107], and the document held to be a demand guarantee, despite the absence of element (iv) above.

In the *Wuhan v Emporiki Bank*'s case mentioned above, there was this postscript that: "... if, on the assumption that the Bank is liable to pay and does pay the amount guaranteed, the underlying position turns out to be that the Buyer never was obliged under the ship-building contract to pay the second instalment. Would the Seller [shipbuilder] hold the amount paid by the Bank on constructive or resulting trust for the Buyer? That is better considered when finality is reached in the arbitration." At a subsequent hearing[108], the COA, held that even though the arbitration tribunal decided that the buyer was not obligated to pay the second instalment at the point in time of shipbuilder's demand, the second instalment was due from the

---

[106] *Howe Richardson v Polimex [1978] 1 Lloyd's Rep 161, Edward Owen v Barclays Bank [1978] QB 159 and Esal (Commodities) Ltd v Oriental Credit Ltd [1985] 2 Lloyd's Rep 546*
[107] *[2002] 1 Lloyd's Rep 617 at para 16.*
[108] *Wuhan Guoyu Logistics Group Co Ltd and Another v Emporiki Bank of Greece SA [2013] EWCA Civ 1679,*

bank under the guarantee because the shipbuilder asserted in good faith that the buyer was in default of payment under the shipbuilding contract. And once payment is due under the guarantee, it remained due. Also, the CoA concluded that the second instalment paid by the bank to the shipbuilder under the guarantee was not held by the shipbuilder on trust for the bank. Also, the CoA considers it inappropriate and declined to express any view on whether the shipbuilder holds the money on trust for the buyer as the buyer was not before the court and: "...the creation of a trust for the Buyer will be inconsistent with the obligation to account which envisages the payment of the balance due on striking the account as between Seller [shipbuilder] and Buyer."

46. Do presumptions in guarantees apply to parent companies?

In *Shanghai Shipyard Company Ltd v Reignwood International Investment (Group) Co. Ltd*[109], involving a shipbuilding contract for an offshore drillship, the court had to decide whether a payment guarantee provided by Reignwood to the Shipyard was a surety or 'see to it" guarantee or a demand guarantee. The terms of the guarantee included, inter alia the following:

- Under Clauses 1, 3 and 10, that Reignwood irrevocably, absolutely, and unconditionally guaranteed "as the primary obligor and not merely as the surety" payment of the delivery instalment and interest thereon at a rate of 5% (capped per clause 10 to a maximum of 60 days interest).
- Under Clause 4, that if the buyer fails to pay the Final instalment or any interest thereon for a period of 15 days, then, upon receipt of the shipyard's first written demand, Reignwood shall immediately pay to shipyard all unpaid Final instalment with the interest. If there is a dispute between the parties concerning

[109] *[2020] EWHC 803 (Comm), [2021] EWCA Civ 1147.*

payment of the final instalment and such dispute is submitted to arbitration, then Reignwood is entitled to withhold payment until publication of an award ordering the buyer to pay the delivery instalment.

- Clause 7 comprised anti-discharge provisions.

Subsequently, Reignwood novated the contract to Opus Tiger 1 Pte Ltd ("OT1"), a single-purpose company. In due course, OT1 refused to pay the final instalment. They contended that the vessel was not in a deliverable condition because of major and critical defects. The Shipyard demanded payment under the guarantee, but Reignwood refused to pay. The Shipyard then sued Reignwood in the commercial court. (Some months later, Reignwood started arbitration against the Shipyard in the name of OT1). The commercial court concluded that the guarantee was a "see to it" guarantee, and not a demand guarantee. It held that under clause 4 the guarantor could refuse payment pending and until the arbitration award. On appeal, the CoA unanimously overruled the commercial court. They stated that the guarantee was a demand guarantee for the following reasons:

- The words "absolutely and unconditionally" in clauses 1 and 3 would convey to a businessman that the obligations were not conditional on the liability of the Buyer.
- The words in clause 1 "[as primary obligor] and not merely as the surety" clearly indicates that the document is not a surety guarantee.
- The words in clause 4 "upon receipt by us of your first written demand" which triggers the obligation to pay "is the hallmark of a demand guarantee. For "see to it" or surety guarantee, the guarantor will need time to investigate whether there was indeed an underlying liability before making the final instalment payment under the shipbuilding contract.

- Clause 10 which limited the interest payable to 60 days, indicates that prompt payment on demand was required, and "not the lengthy delay which might be contemplated to resolve a dispute about the buyer's liability."

The CoA also concluded that as the demand has been made before the commencement of arbitration proceeding, the Shipyard has an accrued right to payment under the guarantee, "immediately upon a valid demand." The CoA also addressed the subject about presumption[110]and reliance on precedents. Regarding presumption, Reignwood had argued that as it was neither a bank, nor a financial institution akin to a bank, but merely a parent, there is this "presumption about the nature of the guarantee which might lead to a different conclusion to that which would follow if a bank had issued it, by reference to the application of different starting presumptions." The CoA rejected Reignwood's argument and stated that:

- It has long been established that payment and refund guarantees may be demand guarantees, and the counterparty risk aspect of such guarantees, is that the beneficiary will therefore look to a guarantee from a bank or other financial institution; or a related party, such as a parent company based on the "commercial and financial strength and probity of the guarantor."
- No preconceptions or assumptions should be made as to the nature of the guarantee based on the identity of the guarantor, as what matters is the wording of the guarantee, "interpreted in accordance with the well-established rules of construction." Otherwise, this would lead to an uncommercial result.
- Even though Reignwood was a parent company and not a bank, this was not significant because Reignwood clearly exercised a

[110] *See: Wuhan Guoyu Logistics Group Co Ltd and Another v Emporiki Bank of Greece SA, supra.*

financing function which went beyond that which would normally arise between parent and subsidiary.

- Regarding reliance on decided cases on traditional and demand guarantee, the CoA stated that similarly worded instruments in such cases are only of assistance if the words used in the instrument "taken as a whole are materially identical; and if the contractual context in which they are used is materially identical."

47. How are the nature of an insurance bonds construed?

In *Havila Kystruten AS v Abarca Companhia de Seguros SA*[111], concerning the termination of two shipbuilding contracts ("SBC") for the design and build of two coastal passenger vessels, one of the issues before the court was whether the insurance bonds were payable on demand or surety bonds. The insurers submitted was that the instruments were not demand bonds for the following reasons:

- There were no words like absolutely and unconditionally, primary obligor, first written demand, and immediate payment in the bonds.
- Insurer was not required to pay "upon the buyer's written demand."
- The word "Loss" in the bonds "means a situation in which the shipbuilder is obliged to reimburse to buyer the instalments paid. Therefore, the liability of the insurer to pay under the bond is only triggered if the shipbuilder is itself liable to repay the buyer.
- The words in bonds requiring the insurer to pay "monetary compensation" to the buyer are inconsistent with a primary obligation to pay and reflective of a liability only if the buyer suffers a loss.

---

[111] *[2022] EWHC 3196 (Comm).*

- The bonds refer to the buyer "making a claim" under the policy. If the bonds were on-demand guarantees, the language should be making a 'demand,' instead of a 'claim."
- If the buyer makes a claim and the shipbuilder disputes liability to repay the pre-paid sums to the buyer, then the buyer's only option is to obtain a final and non-appealable decision from the court.
- The bonds do not provide that the obligations of the guarantor remain unaffected by any dispute under the SBC.
- Thus, the buyer's right to the instalments must be undisputed or judicially determined under the SBC before the insurance bonds respond.

Mr. Justice Henshaw decided that the bonds were on demand bonds. This was because when the bonds are read as a whole, they revealed that the insurer's obligation to pay is not dependent on the buyer establishing any underlying liability on the part of the shipbuilder to the buyer.

48. What is the risk of not verifying a bank's signatory authority?

In *Sea Emerald SA v Prominvestbank*[112], the shipbuilding contract was between a Ukrainian shipyard and a Panamanian buyer. The shipyard provided a bank refund guarantee (governed by English law) to the buyer. The bank's head office was in Kiev, Ukraine. The guarantee was signed by Mr. S, the head of the Nikolaev regional department of the bank. The buyer rescinded the contract because of the shipyard's default and demanded payment from the bank under the guarantee. The bank refused to pay, and argued before the English commercial court that the guarantee was invalid as Mr. S had no authority to enter the guarantee on the bank's behalf. The question of

112 *[2008] EWHC 1979 (Comm).*

Mr. S's authority to issue the guarantee was governed by Ukrainian law. The Buyer contended that "(i) that Mr. S had actual authority; (ii) that his action was ratified by the Bank; and (iii) that he had ostensible authority."

However, the judge found that Mr. S had no actual authority under the bank's article of association to issue refund guarantee on the bank's behalf; no inferred actual authority was conferred on Mr. S by the Management Board of the bank or a relevant power of attorney; and the bank had not ratified Mr. S's act, as there was no evidence to show that such act was adopted by the Chairman or Management Board of the Bank. Note: This case highlights the prudence of only accepting guarantees from reputable international banks; and verifying the bank signatory's authority to issue refund or payment guarantees. This may be done by examining the bank's authorised signatory book or a copy of its duly notarised board resolution.

49. How are guarantees with two possible meanings construed?

In *Rainy Sky SA v Kookmin Bank*[113], it was held that where the language in the refund guarantee had two possible meanings, the court will prefer the construction which is consistent with business common sense. Rainy Sky and others (buyers) signed shipbuilding contracts with the shipbuilder for the construction and sale of one vessel to Rainy Sky and each of the buyers at the cost of US$33,300,000 per vessel. The contracts provided that:

- Before payment of the first instalment, the shipbuilder must provide the buyers with refund guarantees from a first-class Korean bank. Article X.8.

---

[113] *[2011] UKSC 50, [2010] EWCA Civ 582.*

- The buyers shall have a right to a full refund if the buyers exercised their right to reject the vessel or to terminate, cancel or rescind the contract. Article X.5.
- If the shipbuilder is subject to insolvency proceedings, the buyers may require the shipbuilder to immediately refund to buyer the full amount of all sums paid. Article XII.3.

In due course, Kookmin Bank issued identical advance payment bonds ('the Bonds') on the shipbuilder's behalf to each of the buyers. The relevant terms of the bonds stated under:

- Paragraph 2 that under the terms of the contract, the buyer was entitled to a refund if they exercised their right to reject the vessel or to terminate, cancel or rescind the contract.
- Paragraph 3 that in consideration of the buyer agreeing to make the "pre-delivery instalments under the contract", the bank shall pay to the buyer "all such sums due to you under the Contract".
- Paragraph 4 that payment would be made upon receipt of a written demand from the buyer stating that the Builder had failed to fulfil the terms of the contract and specifying the amount claimed.
- Paragraph 5(v) that the bank's liability under the bonds will not be affected by "any insolvency, reorganization or dissolution of the Builder".

Subsequently, the shipbuilder encountered financial difficulties and became the subject of insolvency procedure under Korean Law. The buyers called on the bonds and demanded repayment of the instalments from the bank. However, the bank rejected buyers' demand and contended that:

- They had not guaranteed payment of refunds arising under Article XII.3 of the Contracts (insolvency event).
- The expression "such sums" in paragraph 3 of the bonds was

limited to the sums referred to in paragraph 2 of the bonds when buyers exercised their right to reject the vessel or to terminate, cancel or rescind the contract.

- As paragraph 2 did not include any reference to the buyers' rights under Article XII.3 of the contracts to repayment upon the shipbuilder's insolvency, the bank was not obligated to make any payment to the buyers.

Buyers argued that the words "such sums" covered the "pre-delivery instalments" referred to in paragraph 3 of the bonds, and that means the pre-delivery instalments paid by the buyers. Thus, the bonds guaranteed repayment of pre-delivery instalments under Article XII.3 in the case of insolvency events. The Judge at first instance, Simon J rejected the bank's argument, but a majority of CoA (with Sir Simon Tuckey dissenting), found the bank's argument to be correct.

The UKSC unanimously overruled the CoA. In doing so, Lord Clarke (with whom Lord Phillips, Lord Mance, Lord Kerr, and Lord Wilson agreed) referred to various authorities on the correct approach to construction and stated that where the language used by the parties is unambiguous, then the court must apply it. However, as the language in paragraph 3 is capable of two meanings, the courts should apply "commercial common sense in resolving the question what a reasonable person would have understood the parties to have meant." Lord Clarke also agreed with Sir Simon Tuckey (CoA's appeal judge) that it makes no commercial sense that the bonds would respond to situation where the buyers were entitled to a refund of its advance payments, except for insolvency of the shipbuilder. Further, there were no credible commercial reasons why the parties or the buyer's financiers would agree to this arrangement.

50. What are possible defenses a guarantor might raise?

In *WS Tankship II B.V. v The Kwangju Bank Ltd & Anor.*, [114], the buyer cancelled the shipbuilding contracts as a result of delays and made a demand on the refund guarantee issued by the defendant bank on behalf of shipbuilder. In addition to raising numerous defences, the bank argued that that the refund guarantee applicable in its case is a "see to it" guarantee imposing secondary, not primary, liability, in other words that it was a true guarantee rather than an instrument payable on first demand. The relevant text of the letter of guarantee were as follows:

Letter of Guarantee

Paragraph 1: We hereby open our irrevocable letter of guarantee number…in favour of WS Tankship II.B.V (…"buyer") for account of Geo Marine Engineering and Shipbuilding…, (…"builder") as follows in connection with the shipbuilding contract … made by and between the buyer and the builder for the construction of one (1) one 6,000 dwt asphalt tanker, … (hereinafter called the "vessel").

Paragraph 2: If, in connection with the terms of the contract, the buyer shall become entitled to a refund of the advance payments made to the builder prior to the delivery of the vessel, we hereby irrevocably guarantee the repayment of the same to the buyer within thirty (30) days after demand not exceeding … by telegraphic transfer of such refund.

Paragraph 5: If is hereby understood that payement [payment]of any interest provided herein is by way of liquidated damages due to cancellation of the contract and not by way of compensation for use of money.

Paragraph 6: Notwithstanding the provisions hereinabove, in the event that within thirty (30) days from the date of your claim to the builder referred to

---

[114] *[2011] EWHC 3103 (Comm)*

above, we raceive [receive]notification from you or the builder accompanied by written confirmation to the effect that your claim to cancel the contract or your claim for refundment thereunder has been disputed and referred to arbitration in accordance with the provisions of the contract, we shall under this guarantee, refund to you the sum adjudged to be due to you by the builder pursuant to the award made under such arbitration immediately upon receipt from you of a demand for the sums so adjudged and copy of the award.

Paragraph 7: This letter of guarantee shall become null and void upon receipt by the buyer of the sum guaranteed hereby or upon acceptance by the buyer of the delivery of the vessel in accordance with the terms of the contract.

Kwangju Bank raised the following arguments to support its contention that its guarantee created secondary liability.

- Paragraph 2 of the guarantee: This paragraph starts with the word 'If', thus the provision imposes liability on a contingency. The bank guarantees the "repayment" of the advance payments to the buyer. As GEO is the only party which can repay monies to the buyer, the bank is guaranteeing the performance of GEO's repayment obligation, not promising its own primary obligation. The words "the same" in paragraph 2 refers to the bank's promise to refund the advance payments if GEO is obliged to do so and fails to perform that obligation.
- Paragraph 5 of the guarantee: Refers to "payment of any interest…by way of liquidated damages due to cancellation of the contract…" This shows that liability is secondary, since if the instrument imposed a primary liability, this paragraph would be redundant. Also, the provision mirrors the third paragraph of Article X.5 of the shipbuilding contract, it specifically ties in the obligation to pay interest under the guarantee with the obligation to pay interest under the shipbuilding contract.
- Paragraph 6 of the guarantee: This positively indicates that the

bank's liability is secondary because, if the claim/demand for refund from GEO is challenged in arbitration, the of Kwangju Bank liability is dependent on the determination in the arbitration of the underlying obligations between the buyer and GEO.

- Paragraph 7 of the guarantee: The language in paragraph 7 is consistent with a secondary rather than a primary obligation.
- Finally, the refund guarantee repeatedly uses the words "guarantee" "guarantees" etc. It is also headed "Letter of Guarantee."

Mr Justice Blair held that the guarantee was a demand guarantee and, on the arguments, raised by the bank, stated that:

- The bank's obligation to pay is does not depend on the buyer's contractual entitlement to the refund. The guarantee only requires payment "on demand" against a signed statement certifying buyer's demand in accordance with Article X of the contract and builder's failure to refund.
- The meaning of the paragraph 5 is slightly unclear. A possible construction (by the buyer) is that the paragraph only sought to clarify that interest is not to be treated as a penalty. Though the bank's construction may be plausible, the judge thought it otherwise when seen against the other provisions.
- Paragraph 6 does not imply that the bank's liability is secondary. The instrument is conditioned either upon the certification in the demand, or (if the dispute as to cancellation/refund goes to arbitration) the amount of the award.
- Mr Justice Blair agrees with the buyer that the provision in paragraph 7, is consistent with primary liability.
- The nature of a guarantee depends on the terms of the instrument in question.

In his judgement, Mr Justice Blair also addressed the other issues in the case and stated that:

- The rules as to discharge of a surety, based on material variation or forbearance are not applicable to demand guarantees as the guarantor's liability under the instrument is autonomous of the underlying contract. (See below)
- Disclosure obligation owed by a creditor to a surety has no application to the beneficiary of a demand guarantee as regards the issuer of the guarantee.
- Section 4 of the Statute of Frauds 1677 does not apply to indemnities or demand guarantees. (See below)
- Bank Guarantee sent via SWIFT - An output message header containing the name of a bank generated by the SWIFT messaging system is a sufficient signature for the purposes of the Statute of Frauds. (See below).

51. Does material variation vitiate a demand guarantee?

In *WS Tankship II BV v The Kwangju Bank Ltd and Another*,[115] the bank alleged that the buyers and the yard varied the shipbuilding regard to the timing of the second instalment due under the contract. Thus, the bank is discharged from liability under the principle that a surety is discharged by a material variation to the contract to which he has not consented.

The court held that the rule on discharge of a surety, based on material variation or forbearance does not apply to demand guarantees. The guarantor's liability is autonomous of the underlying contract, thus, disclosure obligation owed by a creditor to a surety is inapplicable to the beneficiary of a demand guarantee.

---

[115] *[2011] EWHC 3103 (Comm).*

52. Does the Statute of Frauds apply to demand guarantees?

In *WS Tankship II BV v The Kwangju Bank Ltd and Another* 5, Kwangju Bank argued that its refund guarantee (which was send via SWIFT message to the buyers' bank,) was unenforceable because it was not signed within the meaning of the Statute of Frauds 1677. Section 4 of the said Statute provides that, "No action shall be brought … whereby to charge the Defendant upon any special promise to answer for the debt default or miscarriages of another person unless the Agreement upon which such Action shall be brought or some Memorandum or Note thereof shall be in Writing and signed by the party to be charged therewith or some other person there unto by him lawfully authorised". The court held that (a) Section 4, Statute of Frauds 1677 does not apply to indemnities or demand guarantees; and (b) bank guarantees sent via SWIFT, with an output message header containing the name of a bank generated by the SWIFT messaging system was held to be sufficient signature for the purposes of the Statute of Frauds.

53. What is the effect of a failure to renew a guarantee?

A delay in renewing refund guarantee may, depending on the facts be a breach of an innominate term and not a repudiatory breach entitling a buyer to terminate the contract. In *Wuhan Ocean and Nantong v Schiffahrts-Gesellschaft*[116], the buyers terminated the shipbuilding contract two days before the expiry date of the refund guarantee on the grounds that the sellers have failed to obtain the extension of the refund guarantee and were therefore in repudiatory breach of the shipbuilding contract. The arbitrators concluded that the sellers were in repudiatory breach of contract as they failed to obtain the extension of the refund guarantee within a reasonable time. On appeal, Cooke J held that there was a breach of an innominate term.

[116] *[2012] EWHC 3104 (Comm).*

Therefore, the buyers were not entitled to terminate the contract based on repudiatory breach. The judge noted that: "…the Buyers did not enquire of the Sellers at any time … as to when the extension would be forthcoming, which would have been a natural and sensible course of action, from which it might be inferred that they were looking to catch the Sellers on the hop and escape their unprofitable bargain. Had they so enquired they would have been told, doubtless, that the extension was about to be given, ... As it turned out there was continuity of security and an extension was given, which demonstrates that the breach was remediable because it was remedied without any prejudice to the Buyers save for the interim uncertainty."

54. When will a call on a guarantee be rendered invalid?

In *Sea-Cargo Skips AS v State Bank of India,* [117] a demand on the refund guarantee issued in connection with a shipbuilding contract was held to be deficient. The guarantee required a statement from the buyer stating that: "(A) that the vessel or the construction thereof is delayed with more than 270 days as set out in the contract article IV 1 (e) which entitles the buyer to cancel the contract and to receive repayment of the advance payments, (B) that you the buyer have pursuant to such right of cancellation duly cancelled the contract…….". The bank contended that the demand failed to make reference to a delay within article IV.1 (e) of the shipbuilding contract, and failed to state that the buyer was entitled to receive repayment of the advance payments. The judge agreed and said that whether the demand was sufficient to trigger the bank's liability to pay was a question of construction, i.e., what did the parties intend would trigger the Bank's liability to pay. The relevant question is whether the demand complied with the refund guarantee and therefore bound the bank to pay. He held that the demand was ambiguous and in the present case did not contain a statement that there had been 270 days of delay as set out in article IV 1(e). Also, the buyer did not state that they were entitled to repayment.

---

[117] *[2013] EWHC 177.*

55. What is the purview doctrine?

In shipbuilding contracts there will inevitably be variations to the specification, plans, drawings, delivery date, and the contract price. Whether such variations can discharge the guarantor's obligation under related payment or refund guarantees will depend on whether such guarantees are a traditional or a demand guarantee. With regard to traditional guarantee, it was held in *Holme v Brunskill*[118], that any material variation of the underlying contract without the surety's consent will discharge the surety from liability under the guarantee, except where it is self-evident that the alteration is insubstantial or beneficial to the surety. This is also because the liability of the debtor and surety under a traditional guarantee are co-extensive. In contrast, the rule will not apply to a demand guarantee, which is payable without proof or condition, independent of the underlying contract and can simply be activated by a demand made on the bank. To circumvent the rule in Holme v Brunskill, some guarantees may comprise anti-discharge provisions to the effect that any indulgence, variation, revision or amendment of the shipbuilding contract, or any extension to the delivery date of the vessel shall not discharge the guarantor's obligations under the guarantee. However, the effectiveness of such anti-discharge provisions will depend on the scope of the guarantee, and whether the purported variation is within the purview of the original guarantee.

In *Trade Indemnity Co. Ltd v Workington Harbour and Dock Board*[119] the terms of the guarantee states that the guarantor shall not be "released or discharged…by any agreement…for any alteration in or to the said works or the contract". A loan which was provided by the employer to the contractor was included in the employer's

---

[118] *(1877) 3 Q.B.D. 495.*
[119] *[1937] AC 1.*

engineer's final certificate.

The House of Lords held that the guarantee did not cover the loan. Lord Atkin said that the words: "...any arrangement...for any alteration in or to the said works or the contract" are very wide. Probably they would have to be cut down so as not to include such changes as have been suggested as substituting a cathedral for a dock, or the construction of a dock elsewhere, or possibly such an enlargement of the works as would double the financial liability.' This was cited in *CIMC Raffles Offshore (Singapore) Limited and Yantai CIMC Raffles Offshore Limited v Schahin Holding*[120], where Sir Bernard Rix said that:

"The effect was that the claim against the guarantor failed, but I rather think that this was not because the guarantee was discharged, but rather because the loan was an entirely extraneous matter."

In *Triodos Bank NV v. Dobbs* [121], Mr Dobbs gave a personal guarantee for loans which was provided by the financing bank for a company's construction project. The original amount under two 1996 loan agreements with the bank were £900,000. This was replaced by two further loan agreements in 1998 and the loan amount increased to £1,980,000. The 1998 loan agreements were subsequently replaced by a 1999 facility agreement which increased the loan to £2.6 million. Clause 2.4.1 of the guarantee contained an "anti-discharge" clause that the bank could:

"... at any time as it thinks fit and without reference to the Guarantor...grant time for payment or grant any other indulgence or agree to any amendment, variation, waiver or release in respect of an obligation of the Company under the Loan Agreement."

The judge at first instance granted summary judgment in the bank's

---

[120] *[2013] EWCA Civ 644.*
[121] *[2005] EWCA Civ 630, [2005] 2 CLC 95.*

favour and held that the guarantee extended to the borrowing under the facility agreement of 1999. Also, Mr Dobbs was estopped from denying that the guarantee so extended.

The court of appeal set aside the summary judgement against Mr Dobbs, leaving the Bank with the option to proceed to trial on the question of estoppel by convention if they are so minded. Longmore LJ stated that (a) a replacement on terms so different from the original agreement…cannot be an "amendment or variation" of the initial contract; (b) any variation (even if there is advance agreement to a variation of the underlying loan agreement) must be within the "purview" of the agreement, and this requirement is still law' and (c) the 1999 facility was not within the purview of the original agreements. Chadwick LJ, on the other hand, considered the issue as one of pure construction, and that:

"…the guarantor is not to be taken to have agreed that his liability under the guarantee would be increased or made more onerous by a subsequent agreement made between the lender and the borrower (to which he is not a party) unless there are clear words in the guarantee which show that he did agree to be bound to a more onerous obligation in the future imposed without further reference to him."

In *CIMC Raffles Offshore (Singapore) Limited and Yantai CIMC Raffles Offshore Limited v Schahin Holding*[122], Sir Bernard Rix left open the question whether the purview doctrine is one of pure construction of particular application to contracts of guarantee, or a doctrine of law, reflecting the equitable concern of Holme v. Brunskill, however much it may be influenced by matters of interpretation. After reviewing various cases, he considers that the purview doctrine applied in two situations. First, it is simply as to its

---

[122] *[2013] EWCA Civ 644.*

scope and either apply or do not apply to the new arrangement. Second, the issue is whether the anti-discharge provision operates to exclude the Holme v Brunskill doctrine.

Reciprocal Indemnity

56. What is the purpose of reciprocal indemnity?

In shipbuilding projects, the risk of loss or damage to property, personal injury including fatal injury and disease are frequently allocated by means of "knock for knock" or reciprocal indemnity in the contract. This means that each party to a contract assume responsibility for loss or damage to their own property or for injury or death to their own employees and identified parties. The rationale behind such indemnity is to avoid protracted litigation, double insurance and most importantly, ensure that "the injured party, or the dependents of the deceased who may have been the sole breadwinner" are compensated timely. In *Caledonia North Sea Ltd v. British Telecommunications Plc Scotland) and others*[123], Lord Bingham commented[124] as follows:

"The position in respect of employers' liability is invariably dealt with by the exchange of mutual indemnities in respect of injuries to or deaths of employees. There is perhaps a simple reason for this. If an individual is

[123] *[2002] UKHL 4.*

[124] *Commenting on the market practice to take account of the peculiar features of offshore operations, referred to an article on the standard practice during construction as described by Sharp, Offshore Oil and Gas Insurance (1994), p 108: "(iv) Injury or Death of Employees.*

injured, he will expect to have a right to sue any party who may have been guilty of negligence, leading to the circumstances which caused the injury. This party may be another contractor, the principal or his employer, or any combination of all three. The issue can become complicated by reason of contributory negligence. Determining liability and awarding costs can be a lengthy process in these circumstances, and this can only add to the anguish of the injured party, or the dependents of the deceased who may have been the sole breadwinner. The employer, therefore, accepts a responsibility to provide for his employees and will generally give the party with whom he is contracting a full indemnity in respect of any suit or action brought against that other party".

Thus, prudent parties in shipbuilding contracts will include reciprocal indemnity clauses where each party assumes primary liability and indemnifies the other, regardless of fault for (a) damage to their own property (and those of their own subcontractors), and (b) personal injuries, disease, or death of their own employees and those of their subcontractors. Such indemnity will typically be drafted to cover members of the shipbuilder group or buyer group as defined in the contract[125]. Liabilities for third party loss, damage or personal injury will usually be to the extent of such indemnifying party's negligence.

As the primary liability assumed by each party will usually be covered under appropriate insurances, each of the party will have to obtain workers' compensation and employer's liability insurance; and comprehensive general liability insurance (personal injury and property damage). The contract will also provide that such insurances

[125] *Shipbuilder group could include shipbuilder and its client, including their parent company, subsidiaries, affiliates and subcontractors of any tier, and their respective officers, directors, agents, employees, and representatives, but shall not include any member of buyer group. Buyer group could include buyer, its parent company, subsidiaries, affiliates, subcontractors of any tier and their respective officers, directors, agents, employees, and representatives but shall not include any member of shipbuilder group.*

must provide (a) for waiver of subrogation whereby the insurer waives all express or implied rights of subrogation against relevant Group, (b) that the policy to be maintained in full force and effect from commencement of construction until the delivery of the vessel, (c) that the policy shall not be cancelled or its coverage reduced except upon prior written notice to shipbuilder and buyer, and (d) the comprehensive public liability insurance provided by should include relevant Group as unqualified co-assureds.

57. Should reciprocal indemnity apply regardless of fault?

The preferred view in some circle is that indemnity clause should allocate liability between the parties, regardless of fault. This ensures certainty, avoids protracted litigation and duplication of insurances. Conversely, others may take the position that the customary reciprocal indemnity or knock for knock regime should not apply in cases of negligence, gross negligence, or wilful misconduct on the part of the party which would otherwise be indemnified. Where a party wishes to avoid liability for negligence under an indemnity clause, the language must be certain and clear. In *Walters v Whessoe Ltd and Shell Refining Co. Ltd* [126], it was held that: "... indemnity will not lie in respect of loss due to a person's own negligence or that of his servants unless adequate and clear words are used or unless the indemnity could have no reasonable meaning or application unless so applied..." per Sellers LJ.

In *Canada Steamship Lines Limited v R*[127], a three-part test was enumerated by the court that: (a) Where a clause expressly exempts a person in whose favour it is made from the consequence of the negligence of his own servants, then effect must be given to such a provision; (b) In the absence of any expressed reference to negligence the court will consider whether the words in their ordinary meaning

---

[126] *1960] CA (Civil Division) 6 Build LR 23.*

[127] *[1952] 1 Lloyd's Rep 1 at p 8, col; [1952] AC 192 at p 208.*

are wide enough to cover the negligence of his own servants; (c) Where the words used are wide enough for the above purposes then the court must consider whether there is another head of damage on which to base the claim other than negligence.

In *EE Caledonia Ltd v. Orbit Valve Co PLC*[128], arising from the unfortunate Pipe Alpha platform disaster in the North Sea), the plaintiffs, EE Caledonia Ltd settled a claim for the death of an employee of Orbit Valve and proceeded to claim reimbursement from Orbit under an indemnity clause. The CoA stated that: "...the prima facie implausibility of a party agreeing to release the other from liability for negligence or assuming liability for the consequence of the others negligence." As the language in the indemnity clause did not expressly cover or excluded loss caused by negligence, EE Caledonia's claim failed as the death was caused by their own negligence. On the question of whether the relevant clause included an indemnity for breach of statutory duty as opposed to negligence, it was held that the clause should be construed as providing that the indemnities are not applicable if the event in question had been caused not only by a party's breach of statutory duty but also by his negligence.

58. Does reciprocal indemnity cover liability to third parties?

As such indemnity only allocates risk between an indemnifier and indemnified party, it will not extend to liability for loss or damage caused to third party. In *Westerngeco Ltd V ATP Oil & Gas UK Ltd*[129], the court reject the contractor's claim and held that the meaning of "liability under this contract" only refer to liability as between the parties to the contract.

---

[128] *1 All ER 174, [1994] 1 WLR 1515, [1994] 2 Lloyd's Rep. 239*

[129] *See infra, Westerngeco Ltd V ATP Oil & Gas UK Ltd [2006] 2 Lloyd's Rep. 535, where the court reject the contractor's claim and held that the meaning of "liability under this contract" only refer to liability as between the parties to the contract.*

Also, if the shares of an affiliate have been given to a bank and registered in the name of the bank, the affiliate will not be able to rely upon the indemnity in the event of a casualty. Thus, in *Farstad Supply A/S (Respondent) v Enviroco Limited (Appellant)* [130], Farstad, chartered their vessel to Asco UK Ltd, (a wholly owned subsidiary of ASCO plc). Under the charterparty, both companies agreed to indemnify and hold each other harmless in relation to certain liabilities. Farstad further agreed to indemnify Asco UK Ltd's "Affiliates." Enviroco (another wholly owned subsidiary of ASCO plc) was contracted to clean the oil tanks of the vessel. In the process of such work, a fire occurred causing the death of one of Enviroco's employees and substantial damage to the vessel. Farstad sued Enviroco for the losses it allegedly suffered. Enviroco relied on the indemnity clauses in the charterparty on the basis that it was an "Affiliate" of Asco UK Ltd because each of them was a subsidiary of ASCO plc. Before the incident, ASCO plc had given the Bank of Scotland security over its shares in Enviroco by registering the shares in the name of the bank (or its nominee). The CoA held that as the shares in Enviroco were registered in the name of the bank's nominee company at the time of the fire, ASCO plc was not a member of Enviroco. As Enviroco was not a subsidiary of ASCO plc it could not rely upon the indemnity clauses. Enviroco's subsequent appeal was dismissed by a unanimous decision of the UKSC.

---

130 *[2011] UKSC 16.*

Consequential Loss

59. What is indirect or consequential loss"?

Most shipbuilding contracts provide for mutual exclusion of liability for indirect or consequential loss. Where the exclusion clause merely refers to "indirect or consequential loss," this will not exclude liability for "direct" losses which fall within the first limb of the rule in *Hadley v Baxendale*[131] . Such clause will only exclude losses which fall within the second limb.

In *Hadley v Baxendale*, the claimant operated a mill. The crankshaft of a steam engine at the mill broke down. As a result, the mill could not operate. The claimant had to send the defective crankshaft to a manufacturer for repair or have a new one fabricated. The defendant was contracted to transport the defective crankshaft to the manufacturer. The claimant did not tell the defendant the mill could not operate while the crankshaft was being repaired or replaced. Due to the defendant's neglect, the delivery of the defective crankshaft to the manufacturer was delayed. As a result, the mill remained closed for longer than expected. The claimant sued the defendant to recover damages. The court held that as the loss of profit

[131] *9 Ex. 341, 156 Eng. Rep. 145 (1854).*

caused by the delay did not flow directly from the breach, the defendant was not liable.

According to the rule in *Hadley v Baxendale*, there are 2 kinds of losses for which a defendant would be liable; (a) loss occurring in the usual course of things, from such breach, (b) loss occurring because of special circumstance where such were within the knowledge or contemplation of both parties, at the time of the contract. Losses outside either of the above are considered too remote and not recoverable. Even though the first and second limbs are commonly referred to as direct and indirect (or consequential) loss respectively, there is hitherto no unanimous definition in the English law context for the term "consequential or indirect loss."

60. What is the modern judicial approach to consequential loss?

In recent times, the CoA doubted whether some of the older cases[132], involving "consequential loss" would be decided similarly today. In *Transocean Drilling UK Ltd v Providence Resources PLC*[133], the CoA had to decide whether wasted spread costs incurred by Providence as a result of Transocean's breaches of contract were "consequential losses" within the meaning of clause 20 in a Drilling Rig Contract. Clause 20 defined Consequential Loss as: "...loss of use (including, without limitation, loss of use or the cost of use of property, equipment, materials and services including without limitation, those provided

---

[132] *Victoria Laundry (Windsor) Ltd v Newman Industries Ltd [1949] 2 KB 528, Millar's Machinery Co Ltd v David Way and Son (1935) 40 Com. Cas. 204, Croudace Construction Ltd v Cawoods Concrete Products Ltd CA (1978) 2 Lloyd's Rep 5, British Sugar Plc v NEI Power Projects Ltd, CA (1997) 87 BLR 42, Deepak Fertilisers Ltd v ICI Chemicals and Polymers Ltd [1999] 1 Lloyd's Rep. 38, BHP Petroleum Ltd v British Steel PLC [2000] 2 Lloyd's Rep 277 (CA), Hotel Services Limited v Hilton International Hotels (UK) Ltd [2000] 1 All ER (Comm) 750, Pegler Ltd v. Wang (UK) Ltd [2000] EWHC Technology, GB Gas Holdings Ltd (Centrica) v Accenture (UK) Ltd & others [2010] EWCA Civ 91, Markerstudy Insurance v Endsleigh Insurance [2010] EWHC 281 (Comm), and Kudos Catering v Manchester Central. [2013] EWCA 38.*

[133] *[2016] EWCA Civ. 372.*

by contractors or subcontractors of every tier or by third parties), loss of business and business interruption". Lord Justice Moore-Bick (with whom the other two Lord Justices agreed) concluded that the language of clause 20 is clear and apt to exclude liability for wasted costs in the form of the spread costs which Providence seeks to recover in this case. In doing so, the appellate court stated that the starting point in construing clause 20 is the language of the clause itself. Clause 20 is nothing like a typical exclusion clause as the parties are of equal bargaining power and have mutually agreed to accept the risk of consequential loss flowing from each other's breaches of contract. The clause is to be seen as an integral part of a broader scheme for allocating losses between the parties as in the knock for knock regime of Clause 18 in the contract. Some of the older cases involving "consequential loss" may not be decided similarly at present as the "courts are more willing to recognise that words take their meaning from their particular context and that the same word or phrase may mean different things in different documents." As for rule in Hadley v Baxendale, it was not necessary to discuss whether the clause derogates from one or other or both limbs of the rule in Hadley v Baxendale as the only question was whether its language is apt to encompass the spread costs.

Also, in *Star Polaris LLC v HHIC-PHIL INC.*[134], discussed earlier under the warranty section, the court chose to differ from the traditional approach by reference to specific wording of the clause in question. A shipbuilding contract between the parties comprised a twelve (12) month guarantee period for defective materials, design errors, construction miscalculation and/or poor workmanship, provided such defects are not caused by inter alia, perils of the seas, normal wear and tear or mismanagement of the vessel and other clauses as stipulated in the Article IX.1. The positive obligations of the shipbuilder were to remedy any defects under the guarantee by

[134] *[2016] EWHC 2941 (Comm).*

carrying out all necessary repairs or replacements at the shipyard, if reasonably practical or elsewhere. [Article IX 3]. Article IX.4(a) provided that the shipbuilder shall have no liability above and beyond its express guarantee obligations.

The vessel suffered serious engine failure some months after delivery and was towed to the shipbuilder's yard for repairs. The buyer alleged that the engine failure was caused by the shipyard's breach of contract and claimed for the cost of repairs to the vessel, towage fees, agency fees, survey fees, off-hire and off-hire bunkers, and diminution in value of the vessel. The arbitration tribunal found that the buyer was entitled to recover its losses for the cost of repairs to the ship under the guarantee. However, the buyer's claim for all other losses, such as associated financial costs caused by the ship's engine failure and diminution in the vessel's value were "consequential or special losses, damages or expenses" in its cause-and-effect sense, and thus were expressly excluded by Article IX (4) (a) the Contract. On appeal, the court held that:

- Consequential or special losses, damages or expenses does not mean such losses, damages, or expenses as fall within the second limb of Hadley v Baxendale but does have the wider meaning of financial losses caused by guaranteed defects, above and beyond the cost of replacement and repair of physical damage.
- The notice provision requiring buyer to give notice of "full particulars of the defect and the extent of the damage caused thereby, but excluding consequential damage, hereinafter provided...," illustrates that there is a distinction being drawn between physical defects and damage on the one hand and consequential damage on the other. [Article IX.2]
- The positive obligations of the shipbuilder are to remedy, at its expense, any defects against which the vessel is guaranteed, by "making all necessary repairs or replacements at the shipyard, if

reasonably practical or elsewhere. [Article IX 3].

- Article IX.4(a) clearly provides that there is no liability above and beyond the express obligations undertaken by the shipbuilder.
- Therefore, financial losses consequent upon physical damage are not covered by the guarantee.
- Also, there is no express provision which gives rise to a claim for financial loss, lost profit, or diminution of value.

Financial cap on total liability

61. What is the purpose of a financial cap on total liability?

A shipbuilder's exposure to liabilities for loss or damage in any given shipbuilding project could be substantial. Therefore, prudent shipbuilder will usually place a financial cap on its total cumulative liability under the contract and at law to a specified percentage of the contract price. As such financial cap operates only to reduce, limit, or qualify the rights of the parties, it is not regarded by the courts with like hostility as those related to exclusion clauses which exclude liabilities altogether.

In Ailsa Craig Fishing Co Ltd v Malvern Fishing Co Ltd[135], the case concerns the loss of two vessels caused by breach of contract and negligence on the part of Securicor (Scotland) Ltd. The issues were whether Securicor liability was limited by a special condition and if so, whether the limit is £1,000 or £10,000. On the question of how such clauses should be interpreted., Lord Wilberforce said that: "Whether a clause limiting liability is effective or not is a question of construction of that clause in the context of the contract as a whole. If it is to exclude liability for negligence, it must be most clearly and unambiguously

[135] [1981] UKHL (12), [1983] 1 All ER 101, [1983] 1 WLR 964, 1982 SLT 37.

expressed, and in such a contract as this, must be construed contra proferentem. I do not think that there is any doubt so far. But I venture to add one further qualification, or at least clarification: one must not strive to create ambiguities by strained construction, as I think that the appellants have striven to do. The relevant words must be given, if possible, their natural, plain meaning. Clauses of limitation are not regarded by the courts with the same hostility as clauses of exclusion: this is because they must be related to other contractual terms, in particular to the risks to which the defending party may be exposed, the remuneration which he receives, and possibly also the opportunity of the other party to insure."

Also, to ensure that such cap is not too wide, most contracts will provide that the cap will not apply to indemnification provisions in the contract, and steps taken by a shipbuilder to fulfil its contract obligations, or to mitigate its own or its subcontractors' delays.

62. Will the cap apply to extra costs for completion of work?

In *Sabic UK Petrochemicals Limited v Punj Lloyd Limited and others,*[136] the Contractor agree to design a plant to produce low density polyethylene for Sabic. Later, the contract was terminated by Sabic due to Contractors' delay.

The contract provides that: (a) if the costs incurred by Sabic to complete the work exceeded the costs that would have been incurred if the Contractor had completed the work as originally planned (without contract termination), Sabic could recover the difference from the Contractor as a setoff or debt. (b) the aggregate liability of the Contractor, regardless of negligence, whether in contract, tort, or otherwise at law, shall not exceed 20% (twenty per cent) of the Contract Price.

---

136 *[2013] EWHC 2916 (TCC).*

On the question of whether the cap on liability applied to limit the claim for the additional costs for completion of the work, the court held that the cap applied only to liabilities incurred for breaches of obligations in contract and tort and not to the claim for additional costs of completion.

63. Does the cap apply to claims by a third party?

In the case of *Westerngeco Ltd v ATP Oil & Gas UK Ltd*[137], the contractor agreed to provide seismic services for the company, ATP Oil. The contract was on industry standard CRINE (now LOGIC) terms, with additional clauses being negotiated by the parties. Under the terms of the contract: (a) the contractor was liable for any damage caused to third parties arising from the negligence of the contractor, (b) the company agrees to indemnify the contractor for any "liability under this contract" that exceeded the aggregate amount of payments the contractor would receive under the contract. During the course of the work the contractor negligently damaged the property of a third party, Total E & P UK Plc (Total). The amount claimed by Total exceeded the amount that the contractor received under the contract. As such, the contractor claims the excess sum from the company under the indemnity in the contract. The court reject the contractor's claim and held that the phrase "liability under this contract" only refer to liability between the contracting parties.

64. Does the cap apply to deliberate or wilful breach?

In *Mott MacDonald Ltd vs Trant Engineering Ltd*[138], the court held that a clause in a settlement and services agreement (SSA),

137 *[2006] 2 Lloyd's Rep. 535*
138 *[2021] EWHC 754.*

comprising a cap on liability, exclusions on liability, and a net contribution clause applied even to fundamental, wilful or deliberate breaches of contract. Pursuant to the SSA, Mott agreed to provide design services for the work being undertaken by Trant in upgrading of facilities at the military base in the Falkland Islands. Clause 1.4 of the Schedule to the SSA provided inter alia, that:

> "...ii) Notwithstanding any other term to the contrary in the Agreement or any related document and whether the cause of action for any claim arises under or in connection with the Agreement in contract or in tort, in negligence or for breach of statutory duty or otherwise. in relation to any and all causes of action as aforesaid: a. the total liability of the Consultant in the aggregate for all claims shall be limited to £500,000 (Five hundred thousand Pounds), and..."

Subsequently, there were disputes between the parties over the scope of work and payment. Mott claimed for payment and revoked the passwords for accessing the building information modelling database, to prevent Trant from gaining access to the design data. Trant alleged that Mott had 'fundamentally, deliberately and wilfully' breached the SSA, by not completing the design deliverables and by failing to provide the native data files and detailed calculations. Trant also counterclaimed for damages and the cost of completing and redoing the design work. Mott denied Trant's allegation and counterclaim, and further contents that even if the breaches alleged by Trant were deliberate and fundamental, the exclusion and limitation clauses in the SSA would still be applicable.

The court held that the exclusion and limitation clauses in the SSA was applicable to any breach by Mott, including fundamental, deliberate, or wilful breaches. In so doing, the Judge went through relevant judicial authorities on the construction of contracts in general, and the approach to the construction of exemption clauses.

The Judge found that the parties accepted the principles governing the construction of contracts in general terms, and reiterated that these principles are to be found in the Supreme Court decision of *Wood v Capita Insurance Services Ltd*[139]explaining the approach taken in *Rainy Sky v Kookmin Bank*[140]and Arnold v Britton[141].

The Judge also reviewed various cases[142] on exemption clauses and provided the following guidance.

- Exemption clauses that purport to exclude or limit liability for deliberate and repudiatory breaches are to be construed by reference to the normal principles of contract construction.
- There is no presumption against the exclusion of liability and no requirement for any particular form of words or level of language to achieve the effect of excluding liability.
- The court should construe the contract to give effect to the parties' intention as disclosed by the language read in context.
- In the absence of clear words, the court is unlikely to conclude that a clause should properly be construed as excluding liability because in those circumstances a departure of this kind from the norm is unlikely to have been intended.
- The nature of the term under consideration will also be relevant in considering the parties' intentions.
- If the language of an exclusion clause is capable of only one meaning, then effect must be given to it.

---

139 *[2017] UKSC 24, [2017] AC 1173.*

140*[2011] UKSC 50, [2011] 1 WLR 2900.*

141 *[2015] UKSC 36, [2015] AC 1619.*

142 *Including Photo Production Ltd v Securicor Transport Ltd [1980] AC 827. Suisse Atlantique Societe d'Armement Maritime SA v N V Rotterdamsche Kolen Centrale [1967] 1 AC 63, and other cases)*

Assignment

65. What is an assignment?

An assignment involves an assignor transferring some or all its rights under a contract to an assignee, so that the assignee is entitled to the corresponding performance directly from and can enforce those rights against the non-assigning party.

Under English law, either party can assign their contractual rights without the consent of the other. However, if the contract stipulates that consent for assignment is required, then such consent must be obtained, otherwise any purported assignment (subject to limitations and exceptions) will be void.[143] In such a case, the consent of the non-assigning party may include conditions that despite the assignment, the assignor (jointly or severally with the assignee) remains liable under the terms of the contract to the extent that it is not fulfilled. To be perfected, notice of any such assignment must be given to the assignee. The assignment does not create a contract between the assignee and the non-assigning party, nor does it make the assignee a party to the original contract.

---

[143] *Linden Gardens Trust Ltd v Lenesta Sludge Disposals [1994] 1 AC 85*

66. Does an assignment include accrued and future rights?

In the absence of clear contrary intention, reference to assignment of the contract by the parties is understood to mean assignment of the benefit, that is, accrued and future rights.

In *Energy Works (Hull) Ltd v MW High Tech Projects UK Ltd*[144], EWHL engaged MW to design, procure, construct, commission and test a gasification power plant, known as the Energy Works Hull Project. Separately, through a subcontract, MW engaged Outotec (USA) Inc ("Outotec") to supply key elements for the construction of the plant. The terms of the main contract and subcontract provided that if required by EWHL, the subcontract could be assigned to EWHL upon termination of the main contract.

- Clause 44.3(d) of the Main Contract provides that upon termination for default: "the Contractor shall, if so, required by the Purchaser and to the extent permitted by the subcontract, assign any subcontract to the Purchaser."
- Clause 9.1 of the Sub-Contract permits MW to assign the Sub-Contract: "…(b) if so required by the Purchaser under the Main Contract the Contractor may assign the Subcontract to the Purchaser."

EWHL terminated the main contract for contractor default and, requested MW to assign MW's sub-contract with Outotec to EWHL. However, MW and EWHL could not to agree to a deed of assignment. Subsequently MW notified EWHL and Outotec that it was assigning the sub-contract to EWHL. O'Farrell J was asked to consider two preliminary issues concerning the assignment and MW's contribution

---

[144] *[2020] EWHC 2537 (TCC).*

claim against Outotec.

The question in respect of the assignment was (a) whether MW retains the benefit of rights under the subcontract, or (b) if otherwise, this takes effect as an assignment of both the benefit and the burden of the subcontract (or a novation). The judge summarized three principles from *Linden Gardens Trust Ltd v Lenesta Sludge Disposals* [145]as follows:

- Subject to any express contractual restrictions, a party to a contract can assign the benefit of a contract, but not the burden, without the consent of the other party to the contract.
- In the absence of any clear contrary intention, reference to assignment of the contract by the parties is understood to mean assignment of the benefit, that is, accrued and future rights.
- It is possible to assign future rights under a contract without the accrued rights, but clear words are needed to give effect to such intention.

It was held that (a) both accrued and future rights under the subcontract had transferred to EWHL upon assignment by MW of the same; (b) the assignment of the sub-contact by MW to EWHL did not transfer the benefit and burden to take effect as a novation.

In arriving at her decision, the learned judge was of the view, inter alia, that the contract and the subcontract simply contained the phrase “assign the subcontract.”

Thus, in the absence of anything to the contrary, the natural and ordinary meaning of this phrase would mean that following assignment of the subcontract, MW assigned all its benefits under the subcontract to EWHL, including both future and accrued rights.

[145] *[1994] 1 AC 85.*

67. May a party assign both contractual rights and liabilities?

While parties may assign their contractual rights (or benefit), the general rule under English law is that they cannot assign their contractual obligations (burden or liability).

If a buyer desires to transfers its rights and obligations in a shipbuilding contract to a third party, the buyer must either delegate, subcontract, or transfer all or part of its rights and obligations to the third party by way of a novation agreement, signed by the shipbuilder, original buyer, and new buyer (collectively "the parties"). The legal effect of such an agreement are as follows:

- The rights and obligations of the original buyer are transferred to the new buyer.
- The parties above must agree to this arrangement, which involved the termination of the original shipbuilding contract and the formation of a new shipbuilding contract.
- Unless the novation agreement is executed by deed, it must be supported by consideration.
- The original shipbuilding contract would have to be valid and binding for the novation to be valid.
- Pre-existing security in respect of obligations; refund guarantee, payment guarantee, and performance bond, under the original shipbuilding contract are automatically discharged and the parties must arrange for issuance of replacement security.
- Where the original shipbuilding contract has been assigned by shipbuilder to its banks, the assignment must be released, and the rights reassigned to the shipbuilder.

68. What are some of the risks associated with novation?

Apart from others, some of these have involved breaches concerning refusal to agree to a novation of the contract; and breach of the arbitration clause after the contract was novated.

In *CMA CGM SA v Hyundai Mipo Dockyard*[146] which involved shipbuilding contracts for four container vessels, HMD refused to consent to the novation of the contracts from the original buyer to CMA (a non-contracting party). CMA sued HMD in tort under Article 1382 of the French Civil Code for the losses which it had suffered from its agreement with the original buyer.

While the French proceedings were ongoing, the original buyer novated the four contracts to CMA, but CMA continued and obtained damages against HMD in the French proceeding. HMD commenced arbitration proceeding against CMA and sought to recover the damages (paid pursuant to the French proceedings) from CMA.

The arbitrator found that CMA committed a breach by continuing to pursue and failing to discontinue those proceedings after the contracts were novated. On appeal, the English commercial court held inter alia, that once CMA became a party to the novated shipbuilding contracts, they were bound to arbitrate any disputes that had arisen after the date of the shipbuilding contracts.

---

146 *[2008] EWHC 2791 (Comm).*

Title to the vessel

69. When can property in the vessel pass?

In most international shipbuilding contracts, title to the vessel will usually remain with the shipbuilder until delivery of the vessel. Under this kind of arrangement, shipbuilder could raise financing for the construction while the buyer will be provided with a refund guarantee as security for its instalments. Alternatively, the parties may agree that title to the vessel will pass to the buyer progressively at different stages of the construction. While this may not affect buyer's right to reject the vessel, the buyer's ability to assert its right to the vessel and uninstalled materials at a foreign shipyard may be limited by the lex situs (the law of the country where the vessel is under construction), when the shipbuilder is under liquidation or insolvency proceedings.

70. When a shipbuilder has title what happens if buyer terminates?

If buyer terminates, some contracts may provide that the shipbuilder must (a) refund all sums paid by buyer together with interests, otherwise, the buyer could draw on the refund guarantee, and (b) return buyer supplies to buyer, or pay for the costs thereof.

The buyer could also apply for specific performance, but English courts are reluctant to order specific performance in contracts that require constant supervision in a foreign state. Thus, prudent buyer will call upon the bank refund guarantee, and unless expressly excluded in the contract, also claim for damages. However, if shipbuilder is the subject of liquidation or insolvency proceeding, the buyer will rank as unsecured creditor for its claim to the refund of instalments and the costs of the buyer's supplies. With such challenges, calling on a refund guarantee will be the best option to claw back its instalments. As for the return of the buyer's supplies, buyer may face hurdles identifying the same (unless the buyer's supplies have been stored in a dedicated and designated space) and shipbuilder's liquidators may be hesitant to incur expenses in dismantling and returning buyer supplies that have been affixed to the vessel.

71. If a shipbuilder has title what happens when they terminate?

The remedies available to the shipbuilder could include calling upon buyer's payment guarantee, and in some contracts[147], retention of buyer supplies, and all instalments paid, the right to complete or not to complete vessel and sell it. With regard to the latter, some contracts may provide as follows:

- Proceeds of sale for completed vessel shall be used (a) to cover shipbuilder's expenses in the sale of the vessel, and (b) for payment of unpaid instalments and interest.
- Proceeds of sale for the partially completed vessel shall be used to pay (a) shipbuilder's expenses for the sale of the vessel, (b) all costs for part construction of the vessel less paid instalments and

[147] *See examples in AWES Article 10, Bimco NBC Clause 39(f), and SAJ Article XI, AWES Article 10.*

sums credited, and (c) shipbuilder's reasonable net loss of profit.

- Excess sum to be given to buyer without interest (not to exceed instalments paid by buyer and costs of buyer supplies, if any).
- If proceeds of sale are insufficient to pay sums due to shipbuilder, buyer to promptly pay such sums plus interest to shipbuilder.

72. If title passes in stages, what happens when shipbuilder terminates?

In such a case, the shipbuilder could call on the buyer's payment guarantee if one is in place, claim for accrued but unpaid instalments, retain the vessel, exercise a contractual, statutory, or common law lien over the vessel. Contractual lien can only be exercised if such rights are included in the contract. Under s41 SOGA, an unpaid shipbuilder in possession of the vessel is entitled to retain possession of the same until payment or tender of the price if: (a) The goods have been sold without any stipulation as to credit. (b) The goods have been sold on credit, but the term of credit has expired. (c) The buyer becomes insolvent.

Power to sell the vessel: If the shipbuilder desires to sell the vessel after retaining her, this must be pursuant to a contractual right or statutory lien. Where a shipbuilder retains the vessel under a statutory lien, they can sell the vessel under s48 (1) SOGA. Under s48(3) SOGA, where the goods are of a perishable nature, or where the unpaid seller gives notice to the buyer of his intention to re-sell, and the buyer does not within a reasonable time pay or tender the price, the unpaid seller may re-sell the goods and recover from the original buyer damages for any loss occasioned by his breach of contract. With common law lien, shipbuilder's right is to retain the vessel, but not to sell her. Another action that may be taken will involve the arrest of the vessel[148], provided the vessel under construction can legally be

[148] *International Convention on Arrest of Ships, 1999 (hereinafter "the 1999 Arrest Convention")*

considered a ship. In exercising any of its above rights, shipbuilder must ensure that the exercise of such rights is not wrongful. Otherwise, buyer will have the right to terminate the contract and claim damages.

73. If the title passes in stages, what happens when buyer terminates?

Where title passes to buyer progressively, and buyer terminates, it could possess the vessel in its complete or incomplete state, complete the incomplete vessel at another shipyard and claim for damages suffered. However, if the shipbuilder is in liquidation before the delivery of the vessel, buyer will have to contend with the local liquidators in accordance with the lex situs (the law of the country where shipbuilder is located).

Even if the buyer prevails against the liquidators and the vessel is partially completed, the buyer will only be able to complete the vessel at another shipyard, with substantial lead time and costs implications. Other potential legal problems which the buyer could encounter may include the following: (a) title to items intended for but have not been affixed on the vessel, and (s) supplier's equipment, machinery and appurtenances is subject to retention of title.

74. What happens to uninstalled materials if the buyer terminates?

In *Reid v Macbeth & Gray*[149] clause 4 of the shipbuilding contract provides that title to the vessel and its components will pass to the buyer during construction. Shipyard went bankrupt before the vessel could be completed. Before the bankruptcy, the shipyard

---

[149] *[1904] AC 223 (HL).*

ordered some material for the construction of the vessel. The issue for the court was whether buyer had title to such yet to be delivered materials based on cl 4 of the contract. The court held that the contract was for purchase of a completed vessel. As such, the buyer could not claim the materials, as they were neither affixed to the corpus nor had they been sold as discrete 'contracts of sale' under the Sale of Goods Act.

In *Re Blyth Shipbuilding and Dry Docks Company*[150] the contract provided that after payment of the first instalment of the purchase price, the vessel and all materials and things appropriated for her (the vessel) shall become the absolute property of the purchasers, subject to the lien of the shipbuilder for unpaid purchase money including extras. After paying two instalments, the shipbuilder's debenture. holder appointed a receiver and work on the vessel was discontinued.

The issue before the court was whether buyer could claim that unappropriated, ready to be incorporated materials, which were not affixed to the vessel was their property. The court held that the property in the unappropriated materials had not passed to the buyer because the contract was for the sale of a completed vessel in a deliverable state and not for the sale of its constituent materials.

75. What happens if there is no provision for the passing of title?

Where a shipbuilding contract is silent on the passing of title or property to the vessel, the courts will have to determine the parties' intention per s18 Rule 5 (1) SOGA, which states that:

"Unless a different intention appears, ... Where there is a contract for the sale of unascertained or future goods by description, and goods of that description and in a deliverable state are unconditionally appropriated to the contract, either by

---

150 *[1926] Ch 494 (CA).*

the seller with the assent of the buyer or by the buyer with the assent of the seller, the property in the goods then passes to the buyer; and the assent may be express or implied, and may be given either before or after the appropriation is made."

In the context of shipbuilding, Rule 5 (1) will apply where:

- The contract is for the sale of a future (new) vessel by description.
- The vessel complies with the contract and specification[151].
- The vessel is delivered[152] by the shipbuilder and accepted by the buyer.

Since Rule (5(1) is subject to contrary intention, title will not pass from shipbuilder to buyer if the conditions for delivery are not fulfilled. Thus, if the contract is for a completed ship and the risk of loss is with the shipbuilder until delivery, it was held that and there was no intention to deliver or part with the property until the vessel was completed[153].

---

[151] *Section 61(5) SOGA, provides that goods are in a deliverable state when they are in such a state that the buyer would under the contract be bound to take delivery of them.*

[152] *Section 18 Rule 5(2) provides that "Where, in pursuance of the contract, the seller delivers the goods to the buyer..., and does not reserve the right of disposal, he is to be taken to have unconditionally appropriated the goods to the contract."*

[153] *Barclay, Curle and Co Ltd v Sir James Laing and Sons Ltd: HL 25 Nov 1907*

Confidentiality

76. How is confidential information protected?

Confidential information means information which is private, not publicly available, and entrusted by a disclosing party to a recipient in circumstances which imposes an obligation of secrecy not to disclose or use the information without the disclosing party's consent. Such information [154] could include those passing between shipbuilder, buyer, designers, subcontractors, and service providers. While wrongful use or disclosure of such information are protected by written agreements or contract clauses, orally communicated confidential information are also protected and a party may be liable for breach of confidence under implied terms or equity, provided three elements are satisfied.

In *Coco A.N. Clark (Engineers) Ltd*[155], Megarry J said that the oral information must have the required quality of confidence, was communicated in situations importing an obligation of confidence, and there have been an unauthorised use of the information to the detriment of the party communicating it.

---

[154] *Confidential information may include the design, technical data, process, and know-how provided by one party to the other during a shipbuilding project.*
[155] *[1969] RPC 41 at 47.*

77. When does an equitable obligation of confidence arise?

If confidential information is disclosed during the process of private business discussion, either orally or through correspondences, the recipient must not, directly, or indirectly use or disseminate such information for their own commercial benefit without the disclosing party's express or implied consent. In *Seager v Copydex,*[156] the plaintiffs disclosed to the defendants' representatives an alternative design for carpet grip. The defendants subsequently manufactured and marketed a carpet grip, like those shared by plaintiffs. The court upheld plaintiffs claim for breach of an equitable obligation of confidence. Lord Denning MR said: 'The law on this subject does not depend on any implied contract. It depends on the broad principle of equity that he who has received information in confidence shall not take unfair advantage of it. He must not make use of it to the prejudice of him who gave it without obtaining his consent…"

78. When will confidentiality obligations be implied?

In *Saltman Engineering Co. Ltd v Campbell Engineering Co. Ltd*[157] the first plaintiffs wanted to manufacture certain leather punches. They engaged the second plaintiffs to prepare drawings for the manufacture of tool to make these punches. The second plaintiffs placed an order for the manufacture of the tool with the third plaintiff. The third plaintiff asked the defendants to manufacture the tool and provided the drawings to them. The defendants used the confidential drawings to manufacture leather punches on their own account.

Lord Greene M R said that the defendants knew that the drawings belonged to the first plaintiffs, and that such drawings were provided

---

[156] *[1967] 2 All ER 415.*
[157] *(1948) 65 RPC 203, [1963] 3 All ER 413.*

to the defendants solely for them to make tools for manufacturing leather punches. He held that:

- If a contracting party obtains confidential matter in connection with a contract, the law will imply an obligation to treat such confidential matter as an implied term of the contract.
- If a recipient uses the confidential information, directly or indirectly obtained from a disclosing party without their expressed consent, express or implied, the recipient will be guilty infringing the disclosing party's rights.
- For the information to be confidential, it must, apart from contract, have the necessary quality of confidence about it, namely, it must not be something which is public property and public knowledge.
- What makes it confidential is the fact that the maker of the document has used his brain and thus produced a result which can only be produced by somebody who goes through the same process.

Where equipment and information are given by one party to a recipient solely to enable that recipient to manufacture items to be supplied for a specified purpose, the recipient is obligated to use the equipment and information solely for the intended purpose.

In *Ackroyds (London) Ltd v Islington Plastics Ltd* [158] the plaintiffs engaged the defendants to make swizzle sticks and provided a mould to the defendants for this purpose. During the contract, the defendants used plaintiffs' mould to manufacture swizzle sticks and supplied them to the plaintiffs' principal customer. Further, the defendants also made a similar mould for their own use from

---

[158] *[1962] RPC 97.*

information and experience gained from the contract with plaintiffs. They then use such mould to manufacture and supply swizzle sticks to the plaintiffs' principal customer. It was held that as there was an obligation of confidence on the defendants, and their conduct amounted to a breach of an implied term.

Intellectual Property

79. What are intellectual property rights (IPR)?

Intellectual property rights (IPR) refer to the legal protection given to the creators or owners of intellectual property (IP) through, patents, copyright, and trademarks for a specified duration.

The IPR of a shipbuilder may include the design, specification, plans, drawings, technical descriptions, calculations, test results, data, and process about the construction of the vessel. Buyer's IPR could include the design, technical information and those related to buyer's supplies. As such, most shipbuilding contracts will provide for ownership of IP to be retained by the true owner. For example, SAJ Article XVI.2 provides for shipbuilder to retain:

"…all rights with respect to the Specifications, and plans and working drawings, technical descriptions, calculations, test results and other data, information and documents concerning the design and construction of the vessel…" and the buyer cannot disclose or divulge such information to any third parties without the prior written consent of the shipbuilder, except necessary for the usual operation repair and maintenance of the vessel[159].

---

[159] *See also, Bimco NBC, cl 40 (a), AWES Form, Article 8 (a).*

For IPR created during a shipbuilding project, some contracts may be silent on the matter while other may allocate the rights to inventions, discoveries, and improvements created during a shipbuilding project as follows:

- If inventions, discoveries, and improvements created under the contract is based on the shipbuilder's know-how, invention and independently created, then such rights should belong to the shipbuilder. In such a case, the shipbuilder may grant to the buyer a limited, royalty-free, non-exclusive, non-transferrable licence to such rights. However, such license should only extend to the repair, modification, and maintenance of the vessel.
- If the intellectual property rights are created by the joint efforts of the parties and it is not possible to distinguish their contribution, then the rights in such intellectual property should be jointly owned.
- All technical information regarding the vessel, developed by shipbuilder during the shipbuilding project should belong to the shipbuilder exclusively. In return, shipbuilder should grant a limited, royalty-free, non-exclusive, non-transferable licence to the buyer solely for the repairs, modifications, and maintenance of the vessel.

80. What are the remedies for breach of IPR?

The innocent party could apply for injunctive relief to restrain an offending party from continuing to use the IP of the innocent party pending the outcome of a trial on the substantive claim. In some cases, the innocent party may even be entitled to exemplary damages. In *Salt Ship Design AS v Prysmian Powerlink SRL*[160], Prysmian appointed

[160] *[2021] EWHC 2633 (Comm).*

Salt as their exclusive designer under a contract for the design of a new build cable laying vessel (CLV). Salt also granted Prysmian the right to build the CLV based on Salt's design package. Section 6.4 of the contract provides that:

"The design, data, documents and know-how and all relevant copyrights, patents or other intellectual property rights related to the Scope of Work supplied by the Designer under this Contract shall remain the intellectual property of the Designer, ... The Client may disclose relevant documentation only to its suppliers and employees on a need-to-know basis. The Client is not entitled to send or make available the General Arrangement and/or Building Specification as a complete document to a third party, including any suppliers, but excepting the Yard, without the prior approval of the Designer."

About a year later, Salt's involvement in the design process came to an end. Around the same time, Prysmian concluded a shipbuilding contract with the Vard Group AS for the construction of a new CLV for Prysmian. Vard Group AS appointed Vard Design AS to carry out the design work for the said shipbuilding contract. Subsequently Salt sued Prysmian on the grounds that:

- Prysmian and Vard Design used Salt's confidential information to develop an alternative design for the vessel unlawfully.
- There were striking similarities between the design used by Vard Design and those of Salt's.
- Salt's design work was used as a springboard, with Vard piggybacking on it (and encouraged by Prysmian), to win the design work.
- Prysmian is liable for unlawful means conspiracy161 arising from

[161] The requirements are as follows: a) A combination or understanding between two or more people; b) An intention to injure the claimant. The intention to injure does not have to be the sole or predominant intention. It is sufficient if the defendant intends to advance its economic interests at the expense of the claimant; c) Unlawful acts carried out pursuant to the combination or understanding; and d) Loss to the claimant suffered because of those unlawful acts. Summarized

a combination between Vard, Prysmian and a Prysmian's representative.

Salt also sought relief under the Trade Secrets (Enforcement etc.) Regulations 2018 relating to the appropriate dissemination and publication of the judgment at Prysmian's expense. The court found that Prysmian (a) acted in breach of clause 6.4 of the contract and its equitable obligations of confidence, and (b) committed the tort of unlawful means conspiracy by engaging in blatant misuse of confidential information where it could obtain a ship, built at a much lower cost, by Vard with the benefit of the Salt design. As for exemplary damages, the court held that: "Prysmian's conduct was sufficiently high-handed or egregious so as to, potentially at least, justify a punitive response."

Finally, the court held that the Trade Secrets (Enforcement etc.) Regulations 2018 was applicable as the design constitute a trade secret and the acquisition, use or disclosure was unlawful.

---

and considered by Bryan J in Lakatamia Shipping Co Ltd v Nobu Su and others [2021] EWHC 1907 (Comm).

Insurance

81. What are the typical insurances in shipbuilding contracts?

Insurance is essential during a shipbuilding project for managing risks of injuries and property damage. Therefore, most contracts[162] will specify that the shipbuilder must provide insurance coverage for builder's risk, workers' compensation and employer's liability, and comprehensive general liability insurance (bodily injury and property damage). The builder's risk policy will provide cover for loss or damage to the vessel, materials, appurtenances, buyer's supplies, and specify that the policy shall:

- Name the shipbuilder and buyer group as unqualified assureds.
- Be equivalent to Institute Clause for Builder's Risk Term (1/6/88).
- Include additional coverage for war risks, strikes and earthquakes.
- Not be cancelled or the coverage reduced except upon prior (insert days) written notice to shipbuilder and buyer.
- Specify that insurers waive all express or implied subrogation rights against shipbuilder group and buyer group.
- Be in full force from the start of construction until the vessel is delivered to the buyer.

---

162 *AWES, Article 9; Bimco NBC, Clause 38 (a) NSF, Article XI.2 SAJ, Article XII Insurance.*

The workers' compensation and employer's liability policy to be provided shall be those prescribed by applicable laws, which provide indemnity with respect to employer's liability, with limits as required by local laws, but in no event less than US$ (insert sum) per person.

In respect of the comprehensive general liability (bodily injury and property damage) policy, this will have to cover all of shipbuilder's operations and including automotive insurance, broad form contractual liability coverage and contractor's protective liability, with a combined single limit of not less than US$ (insert sum) for bodily injury and/or property damage per occurrence, with excess liability limits of US$(insert sum).

The latter two insurance policies must adhere to the following:

- Be valid from the start of construction until the actual delivery of the vessel.
- The policy shall not be cancelled, or its coverage reduced except upon prior written notice to shipbuilder.
- Stipulate that the insurer waives all express or implied rights of subrogation against buyer's group.

Additionally, the comprehensive general liability insurance should include buyer group unqualified co-assureds.

Likewise, buyer will have to provide certificates or certified true copies of the following insurance policies to the shipbuilder with text to the effect that (a) the workers' compensation and employer's liability insurance shall be those prescribed by applicable laws, which provide indemnity with respect to employer's liability with limits as required by local laws, but in no event less than US$ (insert sum) per person; and (b) the comprehensive general liability insurance (bodily injury and property damage) shall cover all of buyer's operations and including automotive insurance, broad form contractual liability coverage and contractor's protective liability, with a combined single limit of not less than US$ (insert sum) for bodily injury and/or property damage per occurrence, with excess liability limits of US$(insert sum).

Both the insurance policies will have to adhere to the following:

- Be valid from the start of construction until the accrual delivery of the vessel.
- The policy shall not be cancelled, or its coverage reduced except upon prior written notice to buyer.
- Stipulate that the insurer waive all express or implied subrogation rights against shipbuilder group.

Additionally, the comprehensive general liability insurance must include shipbuilder group[163] as unqualified co-assureds.

82. What happens if a co-assured is not named in the policy?

In *Talbot Underwriting Ltd v Nausch Hogan & Murray Inc (The "Jascon 5")*[164], Consolidated Projects Ltd (CPL) and Sembawang Shipyard Pte Ltd (Sembawang) signed a contract for the outfitting, commissioning and testing of a pipelay construction barge owned by CPL.

Under the terms of the contract, CPL had to arrange builders' all risk insurance that included Sembawang as an additional co-assured and a waiver of the insurers' subrogation rights. However, CPL's

---

163 The contract may define shipbuilder's group as the shipbuilder, their parent company, subsidiaries, affiliates, subcontractors of any tier; and their respective officers, directors, agents, employees, and representatives, but shall not include any member of buyer group. Buyer's group will include the buyer, its parent company, subsidiaries, affiliates, subcontractors of any tier and their respective officers, directors, agents, employees, and representatives, but shall not include any member of the shipbuilder group.
164 [2006] EWCA Civ 889.

insurance brokers, Nausch Hogan & Murray (NHM), failed to inform their insurers to include Sembawang as a co-assured. Subsequently, the vessel suffered flooding. Sembawang repaired the damage caused by the floodings and claim against the insurers under the BRI. The insurers rejected the claim on the basis that Sembawang was not an assured under the BRI. In due course, CPL settled and paid Sembawang US$850,000. Insurers paid CPL US$501,252.80. Sembawang and CPL assigned their rights against NHM to the insurers.

During the trial between the insurers and NHM, NHM argued inter alia, that Sembawang was an assured under the terms of the policy. Cooke J, the judge of first instance decided that Sembawang was not an assured under the policy.

NHM appealed to the CoA and argued that Sembawang was an "additional assured" within the meaning of the clause in the slip which provides: "Including Assured, interest of Mortgagees (and Notices of Assignment in respect thereof), Loss Payees, Additional Assureds and Waivers of Subrogation as may be required." The CoA unanimously rejected NHM's argument and held that Sembawang was not a co-assured under the Builders' Risks Policy.

83. What are the ILU Clauses for Builders' Risks?

The Institute of London Clauses for Builders' Risks 1/6/88 (ILU clauses), published by the Institute of London Underwriters (ILU) is a globally accepted form of insurance coverage for vessels under construction[165]. It is used solely with the MAR form of policy[166] and is subject to English law and practice. The most recent revision is

[165] However, as such standard policies may be limited, it is imperative to ensure that the cover placed is wide enough to protect against likely risks during a shipbuilding project.

[166] MAR: A market term for the form of marine policy used by Lloyd's and the London company market. It is a basic contract from to which the conditions agreed by the insurers subscribing a marine insurance contract are attached.

dated 1 June 1988, the Institute Builder's Risk Clauses (CL. 351). The ILU clauses comprise Section I (A) i, ii and iii, Section I (B) i, ii, and iii ((a) (b), and Section II, 1 to 19. Pertinent clauses include the insurance period, delayed delivery, subject-matter, insurable value, navigation clause, latent defect, faulty design, and exclusions.

Insurance Period

The assured is cover for a stated duration referred to in the ILU clause as the "provisional period." If the vessel is delivered before the expiry of the provisional period, then the insurance cover will terminate on such delivery date.

Delayed Delivery

If the delivery of the vessel is delayed[167] beyond the provisional period, this can be covered at a premium to be arranged, but in no case shall any additional period of cover extend beyond 30 days from completion of builders' trials.

Subject-Matters Covered

Hull and Machinery under construction at the shipyard or other premises of the shipbuilder "within the port or place of construction at which the Builders' Yard is situated and whilst in transit between such locations." Section I (A). The Underwriters' liability in respect of each item under sub-section (A), which is at such locations shall attach from the time the items are allocated per Section I(A) (I) (II) and (III). Machinery under construction "at Subcontractors 'works and at Subcontractors' premises elsewhere within the port or place of construction at which the Sub-Contractors' works are situated and whilst in transit between such locations."

---

[167] *Note: Where work or repairs are carried out on the vessel by shipbuilder after delivery (including late delivery), it is important to ensure that insurance reciprocal indemnity and are in place to cover loss or damage to property (the vessel and appurtenances) and personal injury or death.*

Section I (B). The Underwriters' liability in respect of each item under sub-section (B), which is at such locations shall attach from the time the items are allocated per Section I (B) (I) (II) and (III).

Under sub-section (B), the subject-matter is also covered while "in transit to Builders if the transit is within the port or place of construction at which the Builders' Yard is situated, and at Builders' Yard and at Builders' premises elsewhere within the port or place of construction at which the Builders' Yard is situated and whilst in transit between such locations." Machinery delivered to shipbuilder is covered while it is "at Builders' Yard and at Builders' premises elsewhere within the port or place of construction at which the Builders' Yard is situated and whilst in transit between such locations." The underwriters' liability shall attach from the time of delivery to the shipbuilder.

Insurable Value

The insured value for the subject matter, should be inserted in the relevant box under Section I (a), hull and machinery at the builder's yard, Section I (b), machinery at a sub-contractor's premises, and Section II, machinery at the builder's yard. Such inserted insured value is a "provisional value" and subject to adjustment in accordance with the "insured value" clause in the ILU.

The insured value of the completed ship is deemed to be the final contract price. However, if the insured value, determined as above, exceeds the provisional value, the assured must declare such excess and pay to insurers premium at the full policy rates, and the insurers shall accept their proportionate shares of the increase; or is less than the provisional value, the sum insured shall be reduced proportionately and the insurers shall return premium at the full policy rates on the amounts by which their respective lines are reduced.

Should the insured value exceed 125% of the provisional value, then the limits of indemnity under the insurance shall be 125% of the provisional value, for any one accident or series of accidents arising out of the same event. Lastly, any variation of the value on account of a material alteration in the plans or fittings of the vessel or a change in type from that originally contemplated does not come within the scope of this clause and such a variation requires the specific agreement of the Underwriters.

Navigation Clause

This provides that the vessel movement must be within the port or place of construction and to proceed under own power, loaded or in ballast, as often as required, for fitting out, docking, trials or delivery, within a distance by water of 250 nautical miles of the port or place of construction. If such distance is to be exceeded, shipbuilder must arrange for payment of additional premium. For movement of the vessel in tow outside the port or place of construction, additional premium must also be arranged, and prior notice must be given to the underwriters.

Latent Defect

Clause 5.1 ILU provides that the insurance is against all risks of loss of or damage to the subject-matter insured, caused, and discovered during the insurance period. This includes the cost of repair, replacement, or renewal of any defective part, condemned solely in consequence of the discovery of a latent defect. The insurance does not cover the cost of renewing faulty welds. While the cost of renewing faulty welds is excluded, the meaning of "latent defect" is not defined in ILU.

Defect

This is summarised as deficiency, imperfection, error, or failure. As there is no requirement connected to the cause of the defect, the wording implies that any kind of defect should be covered. It does not matter if the defect is connected to the design, material, or workmanship, and both defects dating back to the building process and defects developing afterwards should be covered. According to Trine-Lise Wilhelmsen: "This must hold also if the defect has the character of inherent vice, which is excluded in MIA sec. 55. If inherent vice should be accepted as a defence against a claim for damage caused by a latent defect, the coverage or latent defects would be more or less meaningless."[168]

Hull insurance for latent defect

Historically, hull insurance for latent defect in the maritime sector was introduced as a result of *Thames and Mersey Marine Insurance Co Ltd v Hamilton, Fraser and Co, Inchmaree*[169], which decided that the breakage of machinery on board a vessel that was unconnected with the vessel being at sea was not a loss covered by perils of the sea.

A steamship, Inchmaree was insured under a time policy against perils of the seas and "... all other perils, losses and misfortunes that have or shall come to the hurt, detriment, or damage thereof of the aforesaid subject matter of this insurance, or any part thereof." During the pumping up of the main boilers by means of a donkey engine, the donkey engine became over-pressurised and was damaged. This was because a valve in the pipeline between the donkey engine and one of the boilers was closed. The claim for the repair cost of the damage was rejected as it was not caused by a peril of the sea or "all other perils" as the peril was not "of a marine character.

This decision was subsequently mitigated by an extension in the first edition of the Institute Time Clauses Hulls in 1888, common called the "Inchmaree Clause"[170]. However, the judicial meaning of

---

168 Trine-Lise Wilhelmsen: Hull Insurance of "Latent defects" at page 17.
169 [1887] 12 AC 484.
170 The modern form of the Institute Time Clauses Hulls (1995), cl 6.2.1 covers damage to the

latent defect was then strictly and narrowly construed.

Faulty Design and latent defect

Loss of or damage to the vessel insured caused and discovered during the period of insurance arising from faulty design of any part or parts thereof is covered by the ILU. However, the cost of repairing, modifying, replacing, or renewing such part or parts, nor any cost or expense incurred by reason of betterment or alteration in design, is excluded. In *Jackson v Mumford*[171] the connecting rod of the starboard high-pressure engine broke because of an error in design. This resulted in damage to the ship. It was held that (a) defect in machinery in the Inchmaree clause meant:

> "a defect of material, in respect of either its original composition or in respect of its original or its after acquired condition," and (b) "the phrase, at all events, does not, ... cover the erroneous judgement of the designer as to the effect of the strain which his machinery will have to resist, the machinery itself being faultless, the workmanship faultless, and the construction precisely that which the designer intended it to be."

A latent defect which becomes patent will not be covered. Only actual loss to the machinery or hull, or actual damage to the machinery or hull caused by a latent defect is covered. In *Oceanic Steamship Co. v Faber*[172] the vessel was insured for "loss of and/or damage to hull and machinery through...bursting of boilers, breakage of shafts, or through any latent defect in the machinery or hull...'.

While undergoing maintenance, a serious crack caused by previous faulty welding was detected in the shaft. The shaft was condemned, and the assured claimed for loss caused by latent defect.

---

subject matter insured caused by bursting of boilers breakage of shafts or any latent defect in the machinery or hull. See also Institute Voyage Clauses, Hulls (1995), cl 4.2.1.

171 (1902) 8 Com. Cas. 61.

172 (1906) 11 Com.Cas.179.

The Court of Appeal ruled that the insurance did not cover the actual machinery within which the latent defect lay, but only losses suffered because of (or 'through') the latent defect. According to Fletcher Moulton LJ: [p 34] The words 'or through any latent defect in the machinery or hull' means only actual loss to the machinery or hull, or actual damage to the machinery or hull caused by a latent defect, and that it does not mean condemnation by reason of a patent defect.

Damage caused by the latent defect must be to another part of the hull or machinery. In *Scindia Steamship (London) Ltd v London Assurance* [173] the vessel was covered by a time policy of insurance, which includes an Inchmaree Clause. During the removal of the propeller, the tail shaft broke owing to a latent defect. The propeller and the tail shaft fell into the dock and the propeller was damaged. The insurers admitted liability for the propeller, but not for the shaft. It was held the insurers were only liable for damage caused through the breakage of the shaft, i.e., the damage sustained by the propeller.

In *Prudent Tankers Ltd S.A. v The Dominion Insurance Co. Ltd., The Caribbean Sea*[174] Robert Goff J stated that the mere fact that the historical reason for a defect in hull or machinery is defective design would not of itself preclude recovery under the Inchmaree Clause. In this case, the casualty was not attributed to wear and tear, but they were fatigue cracks attributed to the way the ship was designed. Thus, the shipowner prevailed. He also considered that "latent" had the same meaning as it bears in contracts of carriage: a defect which could not be discovered on such examination as a reasonably careful skilled man would make. In *RA Houghton and Mancon Ltd v Sunderland*

[173] *1937 1 KB 639.*
[174] *[1980] 1 Lloyd's Rep. 338,*

Marine Mutual Insurance Co Ltd, Ny-Eeasteyr[175], both parties adopted the test for a latent defect laid down by Mr Justice Robert Goff in the Caribbean Sea case.

In *Promet Engineering (S) Ltd v Sturge (The Nukila)*[176] which concerned the mobile self-elevating accommodation and work platform, Nukila, which was insured under the terms of the Institute Time Clauses, including the Inchmaree clause and the Institute Additional Perils Clause. Fatigue cracks discovered in all three legs of a mobile self-elevating platform were so serious that the platform was in danger of collapsing and extensive repair was necessary. The fractures were the result of welds which had not been properly profiled. Concentration of stress which over a period had caused metal fatigue. The fatigue cracks had spread from the weld to the adjoining structures which the weld was meant to hold together. The bad welding amounted to a latent defect. The issue was whether the serious fractures which had developed from that condition amounted to damage to the hull of the vessel or was a mere manifestation of the defect.

The judge of first instance held that there is no coverage under the Inchmaree clause "if all that has happened is that a latent defect has become patent" and concluded that there was nothing which could be characterized as consequential damage to the vessel. He was of the view that the insurer would only be liable if there was damage to a separate part of the hull or machinery and not merely to the defective part, and that a part for this purpose was one which was physically separable and performed a separate function from the other part. The Court of Appeal disagree and held that:

- The extensive fractures constituted damage to the hull of the

---

175 QB Division (Commercial Court) [1988] 1 Lloyd's Rep. 60.
176 1997 2 Lloyd's Rep 146 CA.

vessel caused by the latent defects (the inadequate welds).

- At the commencement of the coverage period there was a latent defect in the welds joining the underside of the top plate of each spud can to the external surface of the leg tube.
- The latent defect had caused minute fatigue cracks in the surface of the tube in the way of the weld which could also be described as latent defects.

The Inchmaree clause

Clause 6.2 covers damage to the subject matter insured caused by bursting of boilers, breakage of shafts or any latent defect in the machinery or hull. The Institute Additional Perils Clause, for hulls, provides that in consideration of an additional premium this insurance is extended to cover the cost of repairing or replacing any boiler which bursts or shaft which breaks, and any defective part which has caused loss or damage to the vessel covered by Clause 6.2.2 of the Institute Time Clauses. However, the additional perils clauses do not cover claim for the cost of repairing or replacing any part found to be defective because of a fault or error in design or construction and which has not caused loss of or damage to the vessel.

Exclusions

This includes a list of exclusions relating to personal injuries, illness, and death of personnel, punitive or exemplary damages, war, strikes, malicious acts and nuclear exclusions.

84. What are total loss and partial loss?

Under the Marine Insurance Act 1906, (the "MIA") losses can be total or partial. Total losses can be further classified into actual or constructive. Actual total loss occurs when the subject matter of the insurance (a) is destroyed; or (b) or so damaged as to cease to be a thing of the kind insured; or c) where the assured is irretrievably deprived of its use. In respect of (b) the test was provided by Lord Esher MR in *Asfar and Co v Blundell*[177], that:

'...if the nature of things is altered and it became for business purposes something else...If it is so changed in its nature by the perils of the sea as to become an unmerchantable thing which no buyer would buy, and no honest seller will sell, then there is total loss.'

As for missing ship, s58 MIA, provides that if after the lapse of a reasonable time no news of her has been received, an actual total loss may be presumed. For all intend and purposes, constructive total loss are considered commercial write-off. The subject-matter insured must be reasonably abandoned, either because actual total loss appears unavoidable or where the costs of recovering or repairing the goods would exceed their value: s60 (1) MIA. Similarly, under clause 13 of the Institute cargo clause:

'No claim for Constructive Total Loss shall be recoverable hereunder unless the subject-matter insured is reasonably abandoned either on account of its actual total loss appearing to be unavoidable or because the cost of recovering, reconditioning and forwarding the subject-matter to the destination to which it is insured would exceed its value on arrival.'

In the event of a constructive total loss, the assured may either treat the same as a partial loss or abandon the subject-matter insured to the insurer and treat the loss as if it were an actual total loss: s61. The tender of abandonment is a prerequisite to a constructive loss claim, otherwise the loss can only be treated as a partial loss.

Notice must be given with reasonable diligence. It may be in writing, or by word of mouth, or partly in writing and partly by word

---

177 *[1896] 1 QB 123.*

of mouth and may be given in reasonable terms to indicate the intention of the assured to abandon his insured interest in the subject-matter insured unconditionally to the insurer. Acceptance of abandonment may be express or implied from the conduct of the insurer and mere silence of the insurer after notice is not acceptance.

When a notice of abandonment is accepted, it is irrevocable. The acceptance of the notice conclusively admits liability for the loss and the sufficiency of the notice. Notice of abandonment may be waived by the insurer and in certain cases unnecessary. Where there is a valid abandonment, the insurer is entitled to take over the interest of the assured in whatever may remain of the subject-matter insured, and all proprietary rights incidental thereto. However, this right is distinct from that of the insurer's right of subrogation.

Any loss other than a total loss as defined in the Act is a partial loss. Where goods reach their destination in specie, but by reason of obliteration of marks, or otherwise, they are incapable of identification, the loss, if any, is partial, and not total. Apart from the above there are three further types of losses, namely particular average loss, salvages charges and general average loss: see MIA s64, s65 and s66.

Termination

85. How can a party terminate the contract?

A party may terminate the contract through performance, mutual consent, or under contractual or common law rights. Regarding the word "terminate", Lord Justice Moore-Bick said in *Stocznia Gdynia Sa v Gearbulk Holdings Ltd* [178] that:

> "The meaning of the word "terminate" depends on the context in which it is used. It is capable of meaning what is nowadays generally called rescission, that is, the discharge of all rights and obligations under the contract ab initio without liability on either side, and is also used in the context of discharge by frustration, but it is most commonly used in commercial contracts in the context of a right given to one party to a contract to treat it as discharged by reason of a breach on the part of the other.

In *Newland Shipping v Toba Trading*[179], Justice Leggatt said that a contractual right to cancel or terminate a contract (these terms generally being interchangeable) arises when the contract says it arises. The general meaning of cancellation or termination of contract, however, is the termination of all the primary legal obligations

---

[178] *Stocznia Gdynia Sa V Gearbulk Holdings Ltd [2009] EWCA CIV. 75, at para 13.*
[179] *Newland Shipping v Toba Trading [2014] EWHC 661 (Comm).*

imposed by the contract for which performance is not yet due.

A shipbuilder's contractual right to terminate[180] may arise in the event of buyer's payment default[181] or buyer's unjustifiable refusal to take delivery of the vessel and on other grounds stated in the contract. Likewise, the buyer may have the contractual right to terminate a contract for convenience; and in case where the delivery of the vessel exceeds a drop-dead date; and where there are serious shortcomings in the state of the vessel, or its performance, and on other grounds stated in the contract. Such other grounds may include, without limitation, force majeure, total loss of the vessel; insolvency of the parties or their guarantors; and failure to provide or renew guarantees or insurances. A contractual right to terminate may also include those set out in *Pacific Ocean Shipping Corporation & another v Sembawang Corporation,* [182], where Article 37.1(e) of the contract provides the owners with the right to terminate the contract by notice if the shipbuilder:

"...e) fails, neglects, refuses or is unable ... to provide sufficient materials, equipment, services or labour to perform ... at the quality specified and at a progress rate deemed sufficient by the OWNERS to provide a reasonable assurance that the WORK shall be completed in accordance with the CONTRACT provisions."

In addition to its contractual right to terminate, an innocent party may also exercise its right to terminate the contract under common

---

[180] *AWES Article 10 Default by the Purchaser; Bimco NBC cl 39 (b) Builder's Termination, NSF Article XII.2 Buyer's Default, SAJ Article XI Buyer's default.*

[181] *Hyundai Shipbuilding v Papadopoulos, supra, where the shipbuilder terminated the contract because the buyer defaulted in the payment of the second instalment, and Azimut-Benetti SpA (Benetti Division) v Darrell Marcus Healey, concerning non-payment of the first instalment for the construction of a yacht.*

[182] *Pacific Ocean Shipping Corporation & another v Sembawang Corporation,* (the "Solitaire) *[2004] EWHC 2743 (Comm).*

law if the other party is guilty of "repudiatory" breach. The term repudiatory breach was succinctly stated in *Newland Shipping v Toba Trading* as follows:

"Under the general law, a party has the right to terminate a contract if the other party commits a 'repudiatory breach'. ... where a party (a) commits a breach which 'goes to the root of the contract' or deprives the other party of substantially the whole benefit of its performance, (b) commits a breach of a term which the parties have agreed will be a 'condition', i.e., a term any breach of which is treated as repudiatory, or (c) renounces the contract by making it clear that it is going to commit a breach of one of these two kinds."

Discharge is not automatic, and the innocent party may elect either to accept the breach and treat all future obligations as discharged or affirm the contract and require the other party to perform the contract. When the contract is discharged, both parties are released from their future performance but the party in default remains liable for any unperformed secondary obligation to pay monetary compensation for the loss sustained by the innocent party[183].

86. Can common law rights to terminate be precluded?

Upon termination, a party can elect to exercise both contractual and common law rights when the consequences of termination under such rights are identical. It is not necessary to specify which right is being exercised if there is no difference in substance between the two rights which are "in effect one and the same"[184]. In *Stocznia Gdynia Sa v Gearbulk Holdings Ltd*[185], the seller contracted to build three bulk carriers for the buyer but failed to deliver the same by its delivery date or within 150 days or by the drop-dead date as stipulated under

183 Photo Production Ltd v Securicor Transport Ltd. [1980] AC 827, 849, per Lord Diplock.
184 Per Moore-Bick LJ in Stocznia Gdynia Sa V Gearbulk Holdings Ltd at para 20.
185 [2008] EWHC 944 (Comm), [2009] EWCA CIV 75.

the shipbuilding contracts. The buyer recovered monies plus interest from the refund guarantor (which has issued a refund guarantee to secure instalment payments on behalf of the seller) in accordance with the provisions of the contracts. Additionally, they also claimed damages at common law.

- Article 10 of the shipbuilding contracts provided that "...The Purchaser shall not be entitled to claim any other compensation and the Seller shall not be liable for any other compensation for damages sustained by reason of events set out in this Article and/or direct consequences of such events other than liquidated damages specified in this Article."
- Article 10.7 provides that: "Upon termination of this Contract by the Purchaser in accordance ... Article 10 or any other provision of this Contract expressly entitling the Purchaser to terminate this Contract, the Seller shall forthwith repay to the Purchaser all sums previously paid to the Seller under this Contract, together with interest ... from the respective date(s) of payment of such sums until date of refund plus the original cost (invoice value) of the Purchaser's Furnished Equipment if any delivered to the Seller."

The seller contended that Article 10 is a complete code setting out the buyer's contractual rights which displaces any right to treat the contract as repudiated at common law. Even if, Article 10 did not exclude such repudiation, it provided an alternative means of bringing the contract to an end, which can be exercised only in accordance with its terms. As the buyer did not elect to treat the contracts as repudiated under the general law, but terminated under expressed contractual rights it cannot claim damages for the loss of its bargain because Article 10 does not provide for it to do so. Buyer argued that seller had repudiated each of the contracts, which had been accepted as terminating the contract. Therefore, it could recover damages for loss of bargain. The arbitrator held that the seller has repudiated the contract by its refusal to perform and rejected a separate argument that buyer had by its conduct affirmed the contract. He also concluded that Article 10 did not exclude buyer's rights, either the right to treat the contract as discharged on the grounds of repudiatory breach or to recover damages for the loss of bargain. On appeal, to the high court, Burton J reformulated the issues as to whether:

- Article 10 is a contractual code which excludes all rights of termination in respect of the events that occurred here.
- The exclusion clause in Article 10 of the contract excludes any claim for damages in respect of what has occurred.
- The termination of the contracts pursuant to and in reliance upon the contractual termination provisions (coupled with the claim in each case made under the refund guarantee) precludes the buyer from subsequently claiming to have terminated at common law.

Burton J rejected the seller's argument on the first and second issues (as the arbitrator did during the arbitration), held in the seller's favour on the third issue, and precluded the buyer from claiming damages at common law for repudiation of the three contracts as buyer has affirmed the contracts and recovered monies together with interest from the refund guarantor in accordance with the provisions of the contracts. However, the Court of Appeal (CoA) unanimously disagrees with Burton J and restored the arbitrator's award. In doing so, Lord Justice Moore-Bick held that Article 10 and the terms of the contract did not exclude the buyer's common law rights. He added, inter alia that if the parties had intended to preclude buyer's common law rights, then there is no reason why the parties could not have agreed that the buyer should have no right to recover damages for loss of bargain, as "The court is unlikely to be satisfied that a party to a contract has abandoned valuable rights arising by operation of law unless the terms of the contract make it sufficiently clear that that was intended. The more valuable the right, the clearer the language will need to be." (At paragraph 21). As the remedy in Article 10.7 was non-exclusive, the buyer was at liberty to pursue a remedy that would ordinarily be available on lawful termination of the contract.

Despite the case above, it is important to note that if the exercise of one right is inconsistent with the exercise of the other because the consequences of their exercise conflict, the innocent party can only exercise one of the rights.[186]

87. When can a buyer terminate the contract for convenience?

Some contracts may provide the buyer with the right to terminate for convenience or without cause. In such a case, unless otherwise stated in the contract, the buyer is not required to give any reason for the termination.

Furthermore, there is also no implied duty of the buyer to terminate in good faith. In *Monde Petroleum SA v WesternZagros Ltd* [187], the court said that there is no general doctrine of "good faith" in English contract law, except where it is implied by law in certain categories of contract, like employment contract and those of a fiduciary nature. For all other categories of contract, such a duty will only be implied if the contract would lack commercial or practical coherence without it and where all the other requirements for implication are met.

Where a party is contractually bound to perform the contract in good faith, the question of whether such expressed provision imposes fetters on a termination for convenience clause was considered in the

---

[186] *Dalkia Utilities Services Plc v Celtech International Limited [2006] EWHC 63 (Comm).*
[187] *[2016] EWHC 1472 (Comm).*

case of *Optimares S.p.A. v Qatar Airways Group*[188]. The claimant ("Optimares") and defendant ("Qatar") entered into Purchase Agreements for Optimares to design, manufacture, sell and deliver seats for various aircraft. ("the Purchase Agreements"). The Purchase Agreements incorporated Qatar's Standard Conditions. Relevant clauses of the Standard Conditions are paraphrased below:

12.2.3. Notwithstanding anything to the contrary, Qatar could terminate these Standard Conditions, the Purchase Agreement and/or any Purchase Order for its convenience and without incurring any liability.
13.1.1. Neither Party shall be responsible to the other Party for any excusable delay (as defined in the Standard Conditions).
13.1.7. Qatar could terminate the contracts if excusable delay lasted or could reasonably be expected to last for more than thirty (30) calendar days.
16.13. The Parties shall act in good faith in performing their responsibilities and obligations, and shall not, save where provided to the contrary, unreasonably delay, condition, or withhold the giving of any consent, decision, approval, agreement and/or any similar acts.

Optimares notified Qatar of "excusable delay" per clause 13.1.1, resulting from the Covid-19 pandemic in Italy and government-mandated lockdown. The next day, Qatar terminated the purchase agreements and purchase orders for convenience under clause 12.2.3. Optimares claimed that the termination was wrongful on the grounds that:

- Qatar's had no right to terminate for convenience, because once excusable delay had been invoked, this displaces the termination for convenience clause 12.2.3.
- If both clauses were available simultaneously, clause 13.1.7 will serve no purpose as it would always be preferable for Qatar Airways to terminate for convenience.

---

188 *Optimares S.p.A. v Qatar Airways Group Q.C.S.C. [2016] EWHC 1472 (Comm).*

- Clause 12.2.3 does not provide an unfettered discretion to terminate but is qualified by the good faith provision in clause 16.13. Thus, Qatar had a "positive obligation to allow Optimares to perform its work, or at least an obligation not to take steps to frustrate it by terminating the contract."
- The termination for convenience right was not exercisable to re-award the same works to another contractor at a lower price.
- Qatar had not paid for and had been unjustly enriched by the valuable intellectual property which it received.
- Optimares should be entitled to lost profits and its costs thrown away, but if the termination were valid, Optimares should be entitled to its costs thrown away. Otherwise, it would be "a commercially surprising bargain for any party to have entered into."

During the trial, Optimares alleged that Qatar's representative made certain representations and demands. In addition, they also asserted spending "millions of euros in costs in progressing the works and was on the cusp of delivering shipsets." Qatar disputed Optimares' allegations and further stated that prior to the contract termination Optimares was guilty of numerous delays." Qatar's also asserted that:

- It had an unfettered right to terminate the contracts for convenience. The co-existence of the right to terminate for convenience and for excusable delays lasting more than 30 day and though Qatar had the option to terminate, this was irrelevant, as it had been agreed that the right to terminate for convenience would be applicable notwithstanding anything to the contrary.
- By focusing on what it considers to be fair or reasonable commercial conduct, Optimares sought to re-write the contracts to restrict Qatar's right to terminate the contracts for convenience.
- However, the purpose of interpretation is to determine what the

parties have agreed, not what the court thinks that they should have agreed.

- The duty of good faith only applies to the "performance of its respective responsibilities and obligations", and not the exercise of termination right.

Mr Justice Calver held as follows.

Clause 12.2.3 provides a right to terminate for convenience and such right was not restricted by clause 16.13. Clause 16.13 requires the parties to act in good faith in the "performance of the subject matter of the Purchase Agreement, namely the obligation to deliver the seats and all associated matters that may require cooperation between the Parties." However, the exercise of a right to terminate for convenience does not constitute a responsibility or an obligation within the meaning of the clause. Also, clause 16.13 is subject to anything "expressly provided to the contrary".

The evidence did not corroborate Optimares' claim that Qatar terminated the contract "purely on the ground of obtaining cheaper price for the work from another. The judge also stated that even if it was so, Qatar was entitled to terminate under clause 12.2.3 in any event. Optimares' argument about unjust enrichment is hopeless as it was clear that the rights in the intellectual property "vested in Qatar Airways at the time of the creation without any additional cost." Thus, Qatar "had a legal right to receive the intellectual property and there is no room for any claim in unjust enrichment as alleged by Optimares."

On the question of fair and reasonable commercial conduct, the judge said that "while commercial common sense is a very important factor to take into account when interpreting a contract, a court should be very slow to reject the natural meaning of a provision as correct simply because it appears to be a very imprudent term for one of the parties to have agreed, even ignoring the benefit of wisdom of hindsight." Also, the judge noted that Optimares had legal advice and were "... keen to conclude the deal with Qatar Airways..."

88. When does the right to specific performance arise?

In addition to the remedies under a contract and at law, an innocent party will also have a right to specific performance. However, where shipbuilding contracts are between parties from different jurisdictions outside the United Kingdom, the English courts are reluctant to grant specific performance. Hirst J explained the reasons for this in the case of *Gyllenhammar & Partners v Sour Brodogradevna*[189], (concerning a shipbuilding disputes) as follows:

"The final issue was as to the need for supervision, or, as the test has been framed more recently, whether the contract has a sufficient definition of what has to be done in order to comply with an order for specific performance. Here, I need say no more than that the voluminous specification shows that this is a very complex contract requiring extensive co-operation between the parties on a number of matters, in particular modifications, optional variations, and, perhaps most important of all, matters of detail (some by no means unimportant) left undefined in the specification. In my judgment, these factors, coupled with the consideration that the work would take place in a foreign yard outside the court's jurisdiction, would tell strongly against an order for specific performance being in principle appropriate in the present case."

89. Can post-termination rights be included in the contract?

It is possible to legislate on how to deal with the installments, owner-furnished equipment (OFE), the vessel and other matters after

---

[189] *Gyllenhammar & Partners v Sour Brodogradevna [1989] 2 Lloyd's Report 403.*

the contract has been lawfully terminated. Samples from shipbuilding industry standard form contracts are summarized below. The word "Seller" or "seller" shall mean shipbuilder.

BIMCO NEWBUILDCON, Clause 39

When the buyer terminates: The seller must refund all sums paid by the buyer with interest, and must also return the OFE to the buyer or pay for the costs thereof.

When the seller terminates: The seller is entitled to keep the OFE and instalments paid. The seller also can opt whether to complete the vessel, and can sell the completed or partially completed vessel, inclusive of OFE already installed or utilized on board the vessel.

- Proceeds of from the sale of the completed vessel can be used to pay the seller's expenses in the vessel's sale, the unpaid instalments and interest.
- Proceeds of sale from the incomplete vessel can be used to pay (a) the seller's expenses in the vessel's sale, (b) the unpaid instalments and interest, (c) all costs for part construction of the vessel, less any paid instalments and sums credited, and (d) payment of the seller's reasonable net loss of profit.
- Excess sums from the sale of the vessel must be paid to the buyer without interest (not to exceed instalments paid by buyer), and OFE not installed or utilized must be returned to buyer.
- If the proceeds of sale are insufficient to pay amount due to the seller, the seller can then sell the OFE (not installed or utilized) and credit any excess to the Buyer.
- If the proceeds of sale are still insufficient to pay sums due to the seller, the buyer must pay such sums plus interest to the seller.

Shipbuilder's Association of Japan (SAJ), Articles X and XI.

When the buyer terminates: The seller must refund all sums paid by the buyer with interests. All obligations of the parties are discharged after the refund has been made. OFE issues are not addressed.

When the seller terminates for payment default: The buyer must pay interest and all charges and expenses incurred by the seller. The delivery date is automatically extended for 15 days. The seller can retain the OFE and all instalments paid, and elect to compete or not to complete the vessel and sell it.

- Proceeds of sale for the completed vessel shall be used (a) to cover the seller's expenses in the sale of the vessel, and (b) for paying unpaid instalments and interest.
- Proceeds of sale from the partially completed vessel shall be used to pay (a) the seller's expenses for the sale of the vessel, (b) all costs for part construction of the vessel less paid instalments and sums credited, and (c) the seller's reasonable net loss of profit.
- Excess sum to be given to the buyer without interest (not to exceed instalments paid by the buyer and costs of OFE if any). If the proceeds of sale are insufficient to pay sums due to the seller, the buyer shall promptly pay such sums plus interest to the seller.

Association of European Shipbuilders and Shiprepairers (AWES), Articles 10 and 11.

When the buyer terminates: The seller must repay all sums paid by the buyer with interests. The seller can sell the vessel either before or after completing the same and keep the sale proceeds.

When the seller terminates: The seller will be entitled to damages for any loss suffered. Furthermore, the seller can sell the vessel to recoup any loss, without prejudice to its other rights.

Norwegian Standard Form Shipbuilding Contract (NSF), Article XII.

When the buyer terminates: The seller must refund all sums paid by the buyer with interest. The seller must also return the OFE or pay for costs of the OFE. Thereafter, the seller will have no liability for any loss suffered by the buyer.

When the seller terminates for payment default: The seller is entitled to compensation for the loss suffered. If the payment default is disputed, there will be no work stoppage if the buyer provides security acceptable to the seller.

Conclusion

While such arrangements are useful in clarifying the party's post-termination position, there will be complications when one of the parties is the subject of insolvency proceeding. In such a case, the insolvency laws applicable to the party that is liquidated will come into play. This may affect the return of the installments and OFE, and the sale of the vessel and its proceeds. Also, the innocent party will rank as unsecured creditors to any monetary claims.

Disputes Resolution

90. How are shipbuilding disputes resolved?

Some dispute resolution clause in a shipbuilding contract may provide for disputes to be decided in the following manner:

- Classification and technical disputes shall be referred to the classification society or a technical expert (collectively "expert"), and the decision of such expert shall be final and binding.
- All other disputes that cannot be resolved at the project manager level shall first be referred to the senior management of both parties for resolution. If no agreement is reached within 7 days of such referral, the disputes shall be referred for mediation.
- If the disputes cannot be resolved at such mediation, then the matter shall be referred to arbitration. (for example, in London and conducted per the London Maritime Arbitrator Association (LMAA) procedures applicable at the date of the start of the arbitration proceedings).
- Judgment on an award by the arbitrators may be entered in any court of competent jurisdiction for enforcement thereof.

91. Can the finality of an expert determination be challenged?

Generally, English law supports the party autonomy and freedom of contract, and its position is that an expert's determination involves a contract between the parties. Therefore, the courts will not interfere with an expert's determination, even where there is mistake in the determination.

In *Campbell v Edwards*[190], Lord Denning said that: "It is simply the law of contract. If two persons agree that the price of property should be fixed by a valuer on whom they agree, and he gives that valuation honestly and in good faith, they are bound by it. Even if he has made a mistake, they are still bound by it. The reason is because they have agreed to be bound by it. If there were fraud or collusion, of course, it would be different. Fraud or collusion unravels everything." Also, in *Jones and others v Sherwood Computer Services plc*[191], it was held that if the contracting parties agreed to have certain contractual disputes determined by an independent expert whose decision shall be 'conclusive and final and binding for all purposes', such an expert's determination can only be challenged on the ground of mistake if it can be substantiated that the expert departed from his instructions materially.

However, cases have shown that despite the general position, an expert determination may still be challenged on various grounds. This includes application to the court for a stay of proceedings on the grounds that the expert determination clause and process purports to ousts the jurisdiction of the court, or is void for, or is in effect an arbitration clause. In cases where the expert has rendered its decision, the finality of such decision may still be challenged based on fraud,

---

[190] *[1976] 1 All ER 785.*
[191] *1992] 2 All ER 170.*

collusion and impartiality, manifest error[192], material departure from instructions, and errors in determination of questions of law[193]. Examples of how these terms have been judicially defined are listed below.

Manifest errors

Include the following: "...oversights and blunders so obvious and obviously capable of affecting the determination as to admit of no difference of opinion[194]; "is one that is obvious or easily demonstrable without extensive investigation"[195]; and "oversights and blunders so obvious as to admit no difference of opinion"[196].

Material departure from instructions

According to the courts: "If [the expert] has answered the right question in the wrong way, his decision will be binding. If he has answered the wrong question, his decision will be a nullity"[197]. Also, if the "expert had committed an error in considering he was prevented from embarking on the task of applying the correct policy. This was an error in interpreting his jurisdiction, or, putting it a different way, was a material departure from the scope of his instructions."[198]

Errors in determination questions of law

Moore-Bick LJ stated in *Premier Telecom Communications Group Ltd v Webb*[199], that ultimately it all comes down to the construction of the contract under which the expert was appointed to act; and "Only

---

[192] *Macro v Thompson [1997] 1 BCLC 626.C, Shell UK Ltd v Enterprise Oil Plc [1999] 2 Lloyd's Rep 456.*
[193] *Barclays Bank v Nylon Capital [2011] EWCA Civ 826.*
[194] *Veba Oil Supply & trading GmbH v Petrotrade Inc [2002] 1 All E.R. 703.*
[195] *IIG Capital LLC v Van Der Merwe [2008] 1 All ER (Comm) 435.*
[196] *Conoco (UK) Ltd v Phillips Petroleum Co (UK) Ltd ([1996] CILL 1204.*
[197] *Nikko Hotels (UK) Ltd v MEPC plc [1991] 2 EGLR 103.*
[198] *Shafi v Rutherford [2014] EWCA Civ 1186.*
[199] *[2014] EWCA Civ 994.*

by construing the contract can one identify the matters that were referred for his decision, the meaning and effect of any special instructions and the extent to which his decisions on questions of law or mixed fact and law were intended to bind the parties."

92. What is the seat of the arbitration?

Under Part I Section 3 of the Arbitration Act 1996, the seat of the arbitration is the juridical seat of the arbitration designated by the parties to the arbitration agreement, or any arbitral or other institution or person vested by the parties with powers in that regard, or the arbitral tribunal, if so authorised by the parties, or determined, in the absence of any such designation, having regard to the parties' agreement and all the relevant circumstances.

The "seat" need not necessarily be the place where the hearings is conducted. The arbitration law of the UK (and in some countries) allows the tribunal to conduct hearings outside the country of the seat without any changes to the seat.

The importance of the choice of seat is that it determines the law (commonly called "curia law" or the "lex arbitri") applicable to the arbitration proceedings. Thus, if London is designated as the seat of arbitration, the UK Arbitration Act 1996 governs all procedural questions and the English courts will have supervisory jurisdiction over the arbitration proceedings.

Judicial decisions in the UK have also considered the seat of arbitration as akin to an exclusive jurisdiction clause. See *Atlas Power Limited and Others v National Transmission and Despatch Company Limited* [2018] EWHC 1052 (Comm.) at para 37 and 38. See, also International Arbitration, The Key Elements, A presentation by Charles Manzoni, at paragraph 24: "Olympic arbitrations that take place during the Olympic Games. The Court of Arbitration for Sport, which derives its jurisdiction from the Olympic Charter and from the entry form for the games completed by the participants, convenes an ad hoc panel to hear arbitrations during the currency of the games. The idea is that the disputes will be resolved within a few hours of them arising, thus allowing the games to continue as far as possible without being held up by disputes. Clearly therefore the panels sit in whatever country the games are held in, e.g., Sydney, Salt Lake City, Beijing, but the seat of the arbitration is always Switzerland (because the Olympic committee is based in Lucerne) and the lex arbitri is always Swiss law."

93. What is the proper law of an arbitration agreement?

In *Sulamerica Cia Nacional De Seguros S.A. and others v Enesa Engenharia S.A. and others*[200] the dispute between Insured (Enesa Engenharia S.A) and Insurers (Sulamerica Cia Nacional De Seguros S.A concerns two insurance policies relating to the construction of a hydroelectric generating plant in Brazil.

The said policies were governed by Brazilian law clause and a jurisdiction clause giving the courts of Brazil exclusive jurisdiction. The arbitration clause in the said policies, provided that the seat of arbitration was to be in London.

Certain incidents occurred and the Insured claimed under the policies. The Insurers denied liability and the parties started proceedings against each other. Insurers commenced arbitration in London seeking, inter alia, a declaration of non-liability. Insured instituted proceedings in the Brazilian courts pursuant to the exclusive jurisdiction clause. Insurers obtained an anti-suit injunction in the English High Court against the Insured.

The Insured appeal to the CoA. In the CoA, where the issue was the choice of proper law of the arbitration agreement, the CA stated that there are two non-controversial propositions which provide the starting point for any enquiry into the proper law of an arbitration agreement.

---

[200][2012] EWCA Civ 638).

First, the proper law of the arbitration agreement in the main contract might differ from that of the main contract.

Second, the proper law is to be determined by undertaking a three-stage enquiry into (i) Any express choice of governing law, (ii) Any implied choice of governing law, and (iii) Which system of law has the closest and most real connection with the agreement to arbitrate. These three stages should be considered in specified order separately as any choice made by the parties must be recognised. Quite often, stage (ii) might merge into stage (iii) as identification of the system of law with which the agreement has its closest and most real connection is likely to be an important factor in deciding whether the parties have made an implied choice of proper law.

The CoA held that although there were powerful factors in favour of an implied choice of Brazilian law as the governing law of the arbitration agreement, two important factors indicated otherwise:

- The choice of London as the seat of the arbitration inevitably imported an acceptance that English law would govern all aspects of the arbitration agreement, including the conduct and supervision of the arbitration proceedings.
- The second factor was "the consequence said to follow from the choice of Brazilian law as the law governing the arbitration agreement. The insured said that it rendered the agreement enforceable only with their consent.

This indicate that the parties did not intend the arbitration agreement to be governed by Brazilian law. Accordingly, the CoA dismissed the Insured's appeal and upheld the anti-suit injunction against the Insured.

In *Enka Insaat Ve Sanayi AS v OOO Insurance Co. Chubb*[201], the substantive contract's dispute resolution clause provided for arbitration seated in London under the ICC Rules, but it had no governing law clause.

The UKSC held (by a 3-2 majority) that the arbitration agreement is governed by the law of the chosen seat of arbitration, as the law with which the dispute resolution clause is most closely connected. They summarised the principles governing the determination of the law applicable to an arbitration agreement in the following situations.

"i) Where a contract contains an agreement to resolve disputes arising from it by arbitration, the law applicable to the arbitration agreement may not be the same as the law applicable to the other parts of the contract and is to be determined by applying English common law rules for resolving conflicts of laws rather than the provisions of the Rome I Regulation.

ii) According to these rules, the law applicable to the arbitration agreement will be (a) the law chosen by the parties to govern it or (b) in the absence of such a choice, the system of law with which the arbitration agreement is most closely connected.

iii) Whether the parties have agreed on a choice of law to govern the arbitration agreement is ascertained by construing the arbitration agreement and the contract containing it, as a whole, applying the rules of contractual interpretation of English law as the law of the forum.

iv) Where the law applicable to the arbitration agreement is not specified, a choice of governing law for the contract will generally apply to an arbitration agreement which forms part of the contract.

v) The choice of a different country as the seat of the arbitration is not, without

---

201 *[2020] UKSC 38.*

more, sufficient to negate an inference that a choice of law to govern the contract was intended to apply to the arbitration agreement.

vi) Additional factors which may, however, negate such an inference and may in some cases imply that the arbitration agreement was intended to be governed by the law of the seat are: (a) any provision of the law of the seat which indicates that, where an arbitration is subject to that law, the arbitration agreement will also be treated as governed by that country's law; or (b) the existence of a serious risk that, if governed by the same law as the main contract, the arbitration agreement would be ineffective. Either factor may be reinforced by circumstances indicating that the seat was deliberately chosen as a neutral forum for the arbitration.

vii) Where there is no express choice of law to govern the contract, a clause providing for arbitration in a particular place will not by itself justify an inference that the contract (or the arbitration agreement) is intended to be governed by the law of that place.

viii) In the absence of any choice of law to govern the arbitration agreement, the arbitration agreement is governed by the law with which it is most closely connected. Where the parties have chosen a seat of arbitration, this will generally be the law of the seat, even if this differs from the law applicable to the parties' substantive contractual obligations.

ix) The fact that the contract requires the parties to attempt to resolve a dispute through good faith negotiation, mediation, or any other procedure before referring it to arbitration will not generally provide a reason to displace the law of the seat of arbitration as the law applicable to the arbitration agreement by default in the absence of a choice of law to govern it."

94. When is the timely initiation of arbitration essential?

In *Nanjing Tianshun v Orchard Tankers*[202] the shipbuilding contract provide that buyer could cancel the contract if delivery was delayed beyond the permitted contractual limits. If seller disputes such cancellation, it must institute arbitration within thirty (30) days of buyer's cancellation and may not refund the instalments advanced by buyer until an arbitration award is handed down. Buyer cancelled the contract because of delay in delivery. Seller disputed buyer's entitlement but failed to commence arbitration within the stipulated timeframe. The Judge agreed with buyer's contention that seller's right to dispute the cancellation is barred as it failed to meet the 30 days deadline.

[202] *[2011] EWHC 164 (Comm).*

Shipbuilding contract checklist

CONTENT

- Contract Date
- Parties
- Recital
- The Vessel
- Classification
- Contract Price
- Payment Terms
- Guarantees
- Plans and Drawings
- Buyer Representative
- Buyer's Supplies
- Office Facilities
- Subcontracting
- Inspection, Test, and Trials
- Delivery
- Delays
- Force Majeure
- Liquidated Damages
- Variations
- Defects Warranty
- Reciprocal Indemnities
- Consequential Loss
- Cap on Total Liability
- Confidentiality
- Intellectual Property Rights
- Assignment
- Title
- Taxes And Duties
- Insurance
- Termination Rights
- Termination for Convenience
- Governing Law
- Dispute Resolution
- Notice
- Health, Safety, and Environment
- General Provisions
- Appendices

95. What is the purpose of a shipbuilding contract checklist?

A contract checklist helps the party creating the contract aligns the contract terms with those in the checklist. Likewise, the reviewing party can use a checklist to decide whether to accept, delete, or add new terms to a contract under review. In shipbuilding contracts such a checklist would include the terms listed below.

Contract Date

- State the date when both parties sign the contract, and even where the effective date of the contract is subject to contingent conditions.
- The contract date should not be post-dated or backdated, as this will affect the validity of the contract.

Party to the Contract

- State the names of the parties, and the nature of their entity.
- Specify their registered address, and nationality[203].

Recital

- State that the shipbuilder agrees to design, construct, equip, launch, and complete the vessel at its shipyard and to sell and deliver the same to the buyer.

---

203 *The identity of the parties should be verified at the pre contract stage, from official documents filed in their registry of companies or equivalent authority. The purpose of such verification is to ascertain the party's legal capacity, to determine their financial standing, and to carry out credit check, litigation, insolvency or winding up search.*

- Specify that the buyer agrees to buy the vessel, pay the contract price, and accept delivery of the vessel from the shipbuilder per the terms and conditions of the contract.

The Vessel

- Describe the vessel to be built, its hull number, type, design, and class notation per the specification and the contract.
- Indicate the principal dimensions and characteristics of the vessel, i.e., its length overall, length between perpendiculars and breadth moulded, depth to main deck from base line, scantling draught, moulded, draught at assigned load line, bollard pull, trial speed, and main electrical/propulsion plant, electrical power, and specific fuel consumption.
- Specify the degree of deviation or tolerance allowed for the vessel's performance and quality.

Classification

- Specify that the vessel must comply with the requirement of specified classification society and regulatory authority.
- Allocate liability for time and costs impact due to changes in any of the said rules and regulations.

Contract Price

- Specify the contract price and type of currency.
- State whether the contract price is a fixed lump sum, and subject to adjustments for variations.
- State whether the contract price is subject to adjustment for currency fluctuation or increase in the price of materials.
- Delete any language which suggest that the lump sum includes items not specifically mentioned, but may be reasonably inferred from or contemplated by the contract or specification[204].

---

[204] *The term "reasonably inferred" is subjective and open to disputes.*

Payment Terms

- State the payment schedule, invoicing scheme, procedure for resolving disputed invoice, method of payment, banking details, payment for variation.
- State shipbuilder's right to interest, suspension of work, termination of contract for late payment of the contract price.
- Decide whether the buyer should have the right set-off or retain any sum from the contract price.

Guarantees

- State whether the shipbuilder must provide a refund guarantee.
- Specify whether the buyer must provide a payment guarantee.
- Decide whether the guarantee should be a traditional guarantee, (also called a conditional or see-to-it guarantee), or (b) a demand guarantee as the nature of a guarantee depends on its wordings.[205]
- Detail the issuing entity (banks, insurers, finance companies, parent company etc.).
- Specify that such guarantees should remain valid until the actual delivery of the vessel or 30 days after an unappealable court judgement or arbitration award, whichever is later.
- Include a draft version of each guarantee as an attachment to the contract.

Plans and Drawings (P&D)

- Specify the timeframe for the shipbuilder to submit P&D for the buyer's approval, and time limit for the buyer to return the P&D.
- State the procedure to follow if the buyer's comment is vague or ambiguous, or the shipbuilder considers the buyer's comment to be a variation.

---

[205] *Under a traditional guarantee, the guarantor's liability is secondary and dependent upon the liability of the principal debtor. On the other hand, a demand guarantee is payable without proof or condition, independent of the underlying shipbuilding contract, and can simply be activated by a demand made on the bank.*

- State the effect of the buyer's approval or non-approval of P&D.[206]

Buyer Representative

- Detail the responsibilities of the buyer's on-site representative.
- Specify the extent and limit of the representative's authority in binding the buyer.
- Outline the shipbuilder's right to request the removal of the buyer representative from the project.

Buyer's Supplies

- Describe the items to be delivered by the buyer to the shipyard,
- Include the delivery date, delivery conditions (new and readiness for installation), handling, loading, and unloading instructions, storage guidelines, inspection schedules, and the procedure for arrival inspection, and steps to address any defects or damages.
- Specify the accompanying shipping documents, product specification, plans, drawings, instructional materials, manuals, test reports, classification, and other certificates.
- State the consequences when the buyer's supplies are delivered late, deemed unsuitable for installation, or are in breach of third-party intellectual property rights.

Office Facilities

- Specify the office and other facility to be provided for the buyer's project team in the vicinity of the shipyard.
- Describe the size of the office area, number of tables and chairs, air conditioning, internet access, email services, photocopying, and any other amenities.
- Indicate the costs for these facilities.

---

[206] *Some contracts may provide that the buyer's comments or approval or non-approval will not diminish the shipbuilder's obligations in respect of any errors or omissions or any of shipbuilder's obligations under the contract.*

Subcontracting

- Indicate whether the shipbuilder is authorized to subcontract specific portions of the contract work.
- Specify the conditions attached to such authorisation.[207]

Inspection, Tests and Trials

- Specify the buyer's rights to inspect and monitor the construction of the vessel, and attendance at test and trials, and the sea trials programme.
- Indicate the procedures for resolving construction, inspection, and trial results conflicts.
- Describe the method of acceptance and rejection of the vessel after such sea trials.

Delivery

- Specify the location, date, and time for the vessel's delivery.
- List out the delivery documents and certificates.
- Outline the arrangement for rectifying minor defects after delivery.
- If non-essential certificates are not available at delivery, specify the time limit for providing the same after delivery.
- State the effect of buyer’s unjustifiable refusal to accept delivery of the vessel.

Delays

- State the meaning of permissible (force majeure and excluded delays), non-permissible, and excessive delays, along with the

---

[207] *For example, shipbuilder shall: (a) act as the principal party rather than as a representative of the buyer, (b) remain obligated to complete and deliver the vessel; (c) ensure that subcontractors comply with the main contract terms relevant to their designated tasks, (d) oversee subcontractor’s activities, (e) assure prompt payment to subcontractors, (f) permit the transfer of subcontractor’s warranty to buyer, and (g) specify in all sub contracts that subcontractors are not entitled to assert liens or maintain ownership rights over any work, services, or items provided for the vessel.*

notification criteria, rights, liability, and limitations linked to each type of delay.

- Specify that the vessel's delivery date should be extended if it is caused by the impact of force majeure events or other excluded delays as defined in the contract.
- Indicate that if force majeure events exceed an aggregate of 180 or specified days, then either party may terminate the contract by written notice; and buyer may terminate the contract if the aggregate of permissible and non-permissible delays exceed 270 or specified days.

Definition of Delays

- Permissible delay means delays caused by the impact of force majeure events and/or excluded delays as defined in the contract.
- Excluded Delays means default or omission by buyer in carrying out its obligations under the contract, including delay caused by late delivery of buyer supplies or part thereof; delay caused by defects or omission in buyer supplies; damage to the work caused by buyer, its vendors or buyer supplies; destruction of or damage to the shipyard or the vessel or part thereof; and buyer's refusal to take delivery of the vessel.
- Force Majeure: Enumerate the force majeure events, the period for which relief is applicable, notification requirements, restrictions, dis claimers, and termination rights. Force majeure events could include any or more events which delay the construction or delivery of the vessel, including (but not limited) to acts of God; governmental control, requisition, lockdown, intervention or interference; terrorist act or threat, war (declared or undeclared) or other hostilities or preparations therefor; blockade, revolution, insurrections, mobilisation, civil war, riots, vandal ism, sabotages; strikes at the national level, lockouts or other labour disturbances; plague, epidemics, pandemics, quarantines, infectious disease; earthquakes, landslides, flood, typhoons, hurricanes, tidal waves, storms or other

severe weather conditions; fire, explosions; utilities supply interruption; collisions or stranding; embargoes, export and import restrictions; and any cause of similar nature to the above beyond the reasonable control of shipbuilder's subcontractors of any tier.

- Excessive Delays: If the aggregate of permissible and non-permissible delays exceed an aggregate of specified days for example, 270 days.

Liquidated Damages (LD)

- Specify the amount to be paid for delays; the frequency of payment, whether it's daily, weekly, or monthly.
- State whether there is a grace peri od; any maximum limit or cap on the LD.
- Indicate whether LD is buyer's exclusive remedy for addressing delays.
- State the LD that will be payable for the vessel's performance excess or deficiency over an allowable margin.

Variations

- Outline the conditions under which a party is entitled to request variation.
- Specify the process for handling these variations and the required documentations.
- State the effect of no oral variation provisions.
- Outline the methods and alternative used for pricing the variation.
- Describe the protocol for resolving disputed variations.

Defects Warranty

- Provide details regarding the extent of coverage, the scope of services included, the warranty period (including any extensions).
- Stipulate the notification prerequisites, the process for verifying warranty claims and related disputes.
- Specify the exceptions, exclusion of statutory and other implied

terms.

- Indicate the pricing methods for repairs performed by authorized third-party (for examples: the rates for repairs or replacement carried out by the buyer at a third-party shipyard shall be at the third party's rate or shipbuilder's published rate, whichever is lower).
- Attached a copy of a warranty bond (if applicable).
- State whether the warranty is assignability.

Reciprocal Indemnity

- Stipulate a provision where the shipbuilder and buyer indemnify each other, regardless of fault or negligence for (a) damage to their own property and those of their own subcontractors of any tier, and (b) personal injuries,·disease, or death of their own employees and those of their subcontractors of any tier.
- Decide whether such indemnity should apply to members of the shipbuilder group or buyer group as defined in the contract.
- State that liability for third-party loss, damage or personal injury will be to the extent of such indemnifying party's negligence.

Consequential loss

- If both parties are exempt from bearing consequential loss, explicitly mention that the shipyard is not responsible for any consequential loss incurred by the buyer, and vice versa.
- The expression "consequential loss" should be defined in the contract as: (a) consequential or indirect loss under English law; and/or (b) loss and/or deferral of production, loss of contract, loss of charter, loss of use, loss of profit, demurrage, in each case whether direct or indirect to the extent that these are not included in (a) above, and whether or not foreseeable at the date of the contract.

Cap on total liability

Specify whether shipyard's aggregate total liability is limit to a certain percentage of the contract price, and the crave-outs or exceptions.

Confidentiality

- State the specific information and documents disclosing party deems to be "confidential information" (including the method for documenting oral and visual information).
- Specify recipient's undertaking to maintain the secrecy of such information.
- Provide examples of prohibited disclosure.
- Include a reservation of title provision to the information.
- Stipulate disclosing party's representation that the information does not infringe any third-party intellectual property rights; exceptions to confidential information.
- State the duration of the recipient's secrecy obligation.

Intellectual Property Rights (IP)

- Stipulate the parties' IP rights and liabilities for breach.
- State that (a) for IP created by the joint efforts of the parties during the project and it is not possible to distinguish their contribution, then the rights in such intellectual property should be jointly owned, and (b) if the IP rights created under the contract is based on the ship builder's know-how, invention and independently created, then such rights should belong to the shipbuilder. In such a case, the shipbuilder may grant to the buyer a limited, royalty-free, non-exclusive, non-transferable licence to such rights, and such license should only extend to the repairs, modifications, and maintenance of the vessel.

Assignment

- Specify the parties' assignment rights.
- If novation of the contract may be intended, attached a draft copy to the draft contract for shipbuilder's review and revision. Otherwise include a provision giving shipbuilder the liberty to revise the terms of any proposed novation agreement, and to add provision stating

that shipbuilder's legal costs for the novation will be paid by the buyer.

Title to the Vessel

State whether title in the vessel will remain with shipyard until the delivery of the vessel or title will pass to buyer progressively.

Taxes and Duties

- The contract must allocate parties' responsibilities for tax and duties in connection with the performance of the contract.
- State that Buyer should also pay for income tax or levy imposed by relevant governmental authority on its personnel, representatives or subcontractors or any tier, in connection with the performance of the contract at the shipyard.
- Where there are import and export tax exemption on buyer's supplies on presentation of prescribed documents to the local tax authority, state that buyer must supply to shipbuilder such documents as may be required by said tax authority, failing which buyer must indemnify shipbuilder for the consequence of non-compliance.

Insurance

- List out the insurances each party is required to provide. This could include insurances for builder's risk, workers' compensation and employer's liability, and comprehensive general liability insurance (bodily injury and property damage).
- Indicate how the builder's risk insurance proceeds will be applied in the event the vessel suffers a partial or total loss.

Termination Rights

Specify each party's contractual rights to terminate, notice provision, cure period, and the effect of termination.

Termination for Convenience

- Specify the buyer's right to terminate the contract for convenience.
- List out the compensation and demobilisation costs to be paid by the buyer to the shipbuilder.[208]

Governing Law

Stipulate the governing law of the contract, i.e., English law.

Dispute Resolution

- Specify the methods for resolution of disputes arising from or relating to the contract, including the forum for dispute resolution, such as expert determination, arbitration, or judicial proceedings.
- For arbitration, specify the language, place, seat of arbitration, composition of the arbitration panel, applicable law, and regulations, as well as the time frame for initiating arbitration proceedings.

Notice

- State the address and name of person to receive written notice.
- Indicate the mode of transmission, language.
- Specify the names and addresses of solicitors authorised to receive arbitration or court process on the parties' behalf.

Health, Safety and Environment (HSE)

- Describe the policy and consequence of non-compliance. State that ship builder.

---

[208] *Buyer shall compensate Shipbuilder for the following: (a) a cancellation charges equal to __% of the contract price, (b) the portion of work completed at the date of termination, (c) the cost of materials and equipment already purchased, (d) any charges incurred by Shipbuilder for cancellation of agreements with its subcontractors or vendor for orders already placed, and (e) The costs of demobilization, storage, securing and protecting the incomplete vessel against loss, damage or deterioration. Effect of Termination: Buyer shall pay the compensation indicated above to Shipbuilder within 3 months of the termination under this clause, In addition, (a) Buyer shall return all guarantees provided by Shipbuilder for cancellation within 5 days after the termination notice, (b) title to the incomplete vessel should only pass to Buyer upon full payment of the said compensation to Shipbuilder there shall be no warranty for the partially completed vessel, and (c) Buyer shall remove the incomplete vessel from the shipyard within a reasonable time, otherwise, storage and other charges will be payable.*

- Specify that shipbuilder, buyer and all their personnel, representatives and subcontractors of any tier must comply with the HSE rules, regulations, and guidelines of relevant government authorities and those specified in the contract.

General Provisions

Include any other relevant clauses or provisions that are specific to the parties or the project, and boilerplates such as third-party rights, entire agreement, no oral waiver or modifications, severability of invalid provisions.

Appendices

S/N	Documents
1	Specification & Drawings
2	Planned Programme
	Exhibit A - Progress Report (PR)
3	Payment Terms
4	Insurances
5	Variation Procedure
6	Buyer Supplies
7	List of Approved Vendors
8	Shipyard Schedule of Rates
9	Builder's Certificate
10	Bill of Sale
11	Protocol of Delivery and Acceptance
12	Waiver of Liens and Claims

Appendix 1. Specification & Drawings

[To attached the latest version of specification and drawings]

The specification will include the detailed work scope, materials required, intent, definitions, and the followings:

General Description
Principal Particulars
Classification
Regulations & Registration
Certificates
Materials & Workmanship
Welding
Testing
Trim & Stability
Dock Trials
Inclining Experiment
Sea Trials
Bollard Pull Trials
Sound Level Readings
Cleaning and Preservation
Drawings
Framed Up Plans
Delivery
Spare Gear
Supervision & Access
Classification Requirements
Change of Equipment

Additionally, the specification will comprise (a) the work, methods of execution and (b) the materials, machineries, and equipment to be supplied, installed, and tested in relation to the followings:

Structure
Accommodation
Wheelhouse & Stores
Painting
Cathodic Protection
Plumbing & Piping
Deck Machinery
Deck Equipment
Safety Equipment
Machinery
Electrical
Main & Auxiliary Engine
Instrumentation & Alarms
Spares & Tools

Appendix 2. Planned Programme (latest version)

Planned Programme (1/2)

(18 months construction period)

	Activity	1	2	3	4	5	6	7	8	9	10	11	12	13	14	15	16	17	18
1	**Effective Date of Contract**																		
	Receipt of Guarantees																		
	Buyer makes 1st Payment																		
2	**Commencement of Construction**																		
	Design & Drawings																		
	Detailed Engineering																		
3	**Procurement**																		
	Plates & Sections																		
	Pipes, Valves, Fittings, E & I																		
	Equipment, Machineries																		
	Crane and Propulsion Auxiliaries																		
	Telecoms, Fire & Safety,																		
	HVAC, Navigation, Deck Outfitting																		
4	**Fabrication**																		
	Hull & Superstructures																		
	Shot-blasting and Primer																		
	Steel Cutting																		
	Keel Laying																		
	Double bottom Fabrication																		
	Blocks & Deck House Fabrication																		
	Blocks & Deck House Erection																		

Planned Programme (Page 2/2)

(18 months construction period)

	Activity	1	2	3	4	5	6	7	8	9	10	11	12	13	14	15	16	17	18
5	**Piping Fabrication & Installation**																		
	Piping Fabrication																		
	Piping Installation & Testing																		
6	**Equipment & Machinery Installation**																		
	Install Main Equipment																		
	Install Machineries & Crane																		
	Equipment, Machinery & Crane Testing																		
7	**Painting & Outfitting**																		
	Outfitting																		
	Painting																		
8	**Launching**																		
	Launching																		
9	**Tests, Commissioning & Sea Trials**																		
	Tests, Commissioning & Sea Trials																		
10	**Delivery of Vessel**																		
	Delivery of vessel afloat alongside wharf																		

Exhibit A. Progress Report (PR)

The 2-weekly PR shall comprise a statement on the status of the following:

Project Issues	
Safety Report	
Progress Status	
Project Progress	
Construction Progress	
Buyer Supplies	
Procurement	
Summary of Variations	
Project Photographs	
Document Control Log	
Technical and Site Queries	
Others	

Appendix 3. Payment Terms

Agreed percentage of the contract price to be paid upon reaching the following milestone instalments (sample).

Milestones		Percentage
1st	Within 5 banking days of contract signing	10%
2nd	Upon placing the order for steel	10%
3rd	Upon the start of steel cutting	10%
4th	Upon delivery of the vessel	70%

Invoice: All invoice must be accompanied by supporting documents and sent to the Buyer for approval. Any invoice that lacks pertinent documents shall not be considered as received for approval until all relevant documents have been received by the shipbuilder.

Disputed Invoice: In the event of any dispute regarding an invoice, the Buyer shall notify the Shipbuilder within seven (7) days of receipt of the invoice.

Undisputed Invoice: The full undisputed amount of each invoice shall be paid within 30 days of receipt, save for the first instalment, which shall be paid upon contract signing.

Late Payment: Shipbuilder shall be entitled to interest at 2% per annum from the day on which payment was due till the date of payment. Where late payment of any undisputed invoice exceeds 45 days from receipt, the Shipbuilder may, after having notified the Buyer in writing, suspend its performance of the Contract until such payment is made. If Buyer fails to pay any undisputed invoice for more than 90 days from its due date, Shipbuilder shall be entitled to terminate the Contract by giving notice to the Buyer.

Payment for Variations: Payment for variations shall be 50% upon signing of the Variation Order and balance upon completion of the variation work.

Banking Details: Save where payment is specified to be by letter of credit, all amounts due and payable to the Shipbuilder pursuant hereto shall be paid by wire transfer to the Shipbuilder's bank account stated below.

Name of Bank:
Account No.:
Swift Code:
Account Name:

Expenses and bank charges for remitting any payments under this Contract shall be for the account of the Payer. Bank charges (if any) levied by Payee's bank shall be for the account of Payee.

Appendix 4. Insurances

Before the commencement of construction, the Shipbuilder and Buyer shall provide certificates or certified true copies of the following insurance policies to each other.

Workers' Compensation and Employer's Liability Insurance as prescribed by all applicable laws, and providing indemnity for Employer's Liability with limits as required by local laws, but in no event less than US$ (insert sum) per person.

Comprehensive General Liability Insurance (Bodily Injury and Property Damage) covering all of Buyer's operations and including Automotive insurance, including broad form contractual liability coverage and contractor's protective liability, with a combined single limit of not less than US$ (insert sum) for bodily injury and/or property damage per occurrence, with excess liability limits of US$(insert sum).

Such insurance policies should provide (a) for waiver of subrogation whereby the insurer waives all express or implied rights of subrogation against each other's Group, (b) that the policy to be maintained in full force and effect by the parties from the commencement of construction until the delivery of the vessel, (c) that the policy shall not be cancelled or its coverage reduced except upon prior written notice to Shipbuilder and Buyer, and (d) the comprehensive public liability insurance provided should include the each other's Group as unqualified co-assured.

Builder's Risk Policy
The Shipbuilder shall from the commencement of construction until delivery of the vessel, procure builder's risk insurance policy, (including protection and indemnity), to cover loss or risk of damage to the vessel, including its materials, appurtenances, and Buyer Supplies.

The Builder's Risk policy shall, either on the face thereof or by appropriate endorsement:

(a) Name Shipbuilder Group and Buyer Group as unqualified assured.

(b) Provide that it shall not be cancelled or its coverage reduced except upon ten days' prior written notice to Shipbuilder and Buyer.
(c) Include provisions whereby insurers waive all express or implied rights of subrogation against Shipbuilder Group and Buyer Group.
(d) Be maintained in full force and effect by Shipbuilder from the commencement of construction until the vessel is delivered to the Buyer on the scheduled or extended delivery date.

The following arrangement shall be applicable where the vessel suffers partial loss or actual or constructive total loss at any time on or before delivery.

Partial Loss. Insurance proceeds received should be used to repair or replace damaged items (including Buyer Supplies), Shipbuilder shall be entitled to any extension of time to carry out the repairs or replacement, and Buyer shall not make any objection on the depreciation of the repaired items or that they are not considered "new" items.

Total Loss. Insurance proceeds received should be used to reimburse Buyer for all instalments paid (without interests), insurance proceeds received for Buyer Supplies to be release to Buyer or Shipbuilder to deliver, at Buyer's expenses, all Buyer Supplies (if any) to Buyer, the contract is automatically terminated and all rights, duties, and obligations of each of the parties to the other shall forthwith cease, and balance of the insurance proceeds shall belong to the Shipbuilder.

As an alternative to terminating the contract in the event of a total loss, the parties may mutually agree to apply the insurance proceeds to build a new vessel or have the damaged vessel rebuilt subject to a new delivery date and other amendments. If no agreement is reached, then the contract shall be terminated and all rights, duties, and obligations of each of the parties to the other shall forthwith cease.

Surveyor appointed by insurers shall determine whether an actual or constructive total loss has occurred.

Appendix 5. Variation Procedure

This variation procedure must be adhered to when (a) revisions are made to the specification and work schedule, and (b) there is a claim for extension of time and/or adjustment of the contract price due to permissible delays or relief under the Contract.

All variation orders must be in writing, signed by shipbuilder's duly authorized representatives and under the procedural requirements in the Contract.

Shipbuilder shall only proceed with any variation work after issuance of a written variation order. The form of the variation order requests shall comprise:

- The nature of the change required.
- A statement of effects with supporting documents.
- Lump-sum price, unit or time and materials pricing.
- Breakdown of labour and materials costs.
- Any changes in the work schedule.
- Total costs for the proposed variation.
- Any other relevant consequences.

The pricing for variation work or supply should be on a lump sum basis. Where the Parties cannot agree on a lump sum, the variation shall be performed on unit or time and materials basis (T & M) based on Schedule of Price & Rates. Materials used in performing T & M work shall be billed at Shipbuilder's net cost plus a 10% mark-up.

Payment for variations performed on a lump sum basis shall be 30% upon commencement of variation work and balance 70% upon completion and acceptance of variation work.

Payment for variation performed on unit or T & M basis shall be monthly.

Pending final resolution of any disagreement relating to the pricing for variations, the Shipbuilder shall continue with the performance of this Contract on a T & M basis.

Disputed Variation

Where there are disputes as to whether the purported variation work requested by the Buyer is within the Shipbuilder's contractual scope of work, the Shipbuilder must carry out the variation work provided the Buyer agrees to pays for the variations in the manner set out above. Such payment shall not prejudice the Buyers's right to refer the matter to arbitration within 30 days after the completion of the variation. work. If it is determined at such arbitration that the variation work is within the Shipbuilder's scope of work, then the Shipbuilder must refund such sums as may be awarded to the Buyer within 14 days of the arbitration award.

Appendix 6. Buyer Supplies

List of Buyer Supplies with scheduled arrival dates (ETA).

.

No	Name	ETA

Appendix 7. List of Approved Subcontractors

No	Name	Discipline

Appendix 8. Shipyard Schedule of Rates

Site Office for Buyer's Representative
USD ________________ monthly/per person
500 square feet office space for 10 people, equipped with air-conditioning, access to internet facility, fax/telex, photocopying, and such other reasonable facilities in the vicinity of the shipyard. International telecommunication charges shall be reimbursed to Shipbuilder at cost +15%.

Manpower Rates & Prices

Normal Rate: Monday to Saturday, 0800 to 1200 hrs and 1300 to 1700 hrs, overtime rate: night shift, public holiday and Sunday shall be 1.5 times the normal rate.

Items	Hourly Rates
Engineering	
Administration	
Site Manpower	
Yard Facilities	
Plants and Equipment	
Mooring and Rigging	
Attendance at Quayside	
Wharf charges	
Mooring and unmooring	
Utility supply and bunker	
Pressure Testing	
Non-Destructive Testing	
Loading and unloading	
Storage for Buyer Supplies	

Materials & Equipment Procurement

Cost for procurement services, expediting, inspection, taking delivery, unloading, handling, third party services engaged by the buyer, costs for procurement, services, financing, use of all facilities including lighting and power, handling and transportation of Buyer Supplies, construction consumables, costs for all field works. All these will be chargeable at Shipbuilder's cost plus 15% mark up.

Appendix 9. Builder's Certificate

Builder Certificate

We, the Builder, (name of shipbuilder) hereby certify that the vessel as described below was constructed at our shipyard at (address) in the year _____ and delivered to the Buyer (name) on (delivery date).

Hull number	
Place of construction	
Length overall	
Breadth moulded	
Depth moulded	
International tonnage	
Class notation	
Build	
Propulsion	
Main generators	
Harbour generator	
Emergency generator	
Number of decks	
Number of masts	
Accommodation	

Signed by Builder and Buyer

Appendix 10. Bill of Sale

Bill of Sale

Shipbuilding Contract dated ___
Hull No.
Name of Vessel (the "Vessel")

Name of Buyer and Shipbuilder

We, [name of shipyard], the shipbuilder, in consideration of US$ [insert amount] and other good and valuable consideration the receipt whereof is hereby acknowledged, do hereby transfer our whole title, ownership and interest in the vessel including the appurtenances and spares to the buyer.

Further, we, the shipbuilder, for ourselves and our successors covenant with the buyer and their assigns that we have the power to transfer to the buyer the vessel and title thereto and that the vessel is free from all encumbrances, debts, maritime liens, mortgages, and any other claims whatsoever.

Dated this _____ day of _______ (year).

Signed by the Shipbuilder

Appendix 11. Protocol of Delivery and Acceptance

Protocol of Delivery and Acceptance

Shipbuilder Letterhead

Shipbuilding Contract dated [insert date) by and between:
Name of Buyer and Shipbuilder

Under clause ___ of the above contract, buyer hereby certifies to the shipbuilder that, subject to any exceptions below, buyer hereby accepts the delivery of the vessel, hull number [ ] under the terms of the contract and hereby instructs shipbuilder to deliver the vessel to the buyer. Nothing herein shall be deemed to constitute a waiver of the buyer's rights under the contract.

Exceptions: The outstanding items listed in the attached Punch List.

Yours faithfully,
Signed by Shipbuilder.

Agreed and accepted this (date) of (month) and (Year)

Signature of the Buyer

Appendix 12. Waiver of Liens and Claims

Waiver of Liens and Claims

Shipbuilding Contract dated:
Hull No.

Name of Shipbuilder
Name of Buyer

Shipbuilder hereby certifies that:

The vessel, identified as Hull No. ____ is free and clear from all liens, charges, encumbrances and claims whatsoever from the shipbuilder, its subcontractors, suppliers, and any other party claiming through shipbuilder. The contract price under the shipbuilding contract has been paid in full and there are no outstanding claims against the buyer in respect thereof. Shipbuilder hereby indemnifies buyer against all liens, charges, encumbrances, and claims referred to above.

Dated this (insert date)

Signed by the Shipbuilder

Subcontractor's Risks

96. How are subcontractor's risks mitigated?

In addition to managing risks in a shipbuilding contract, special attention should also be placed on the shipbuilder's subcontract with its subcontractors and vendors (collectively "Subcontractor(s)"). This is crucial because late delivery or completion, omissions or defects in subcontractors work or supply may delay the construction schedule of the main shipbuilding contract leading to adverse consequences for the shipbuilder and the buyer.

Downside for the shipbuilder

As a shipbuilder is responsible for its subcontractor's delay, the impact of such delay on the main shipbuilding contract will be for the account of the shipbuilder, leading to the following consequences:

- The buyer could claim liquidated damages from the shipbuilder.
- The shipbuilder will not be able to recoup such liquidated damages in full from the subcontractor as liquidated damages payable under a subcontract will usually be lower than those in the shipbuilding contract.
- If the delay is protracted, buyer may terminate the shipbuilding contract.

Downside for the buyer

The buyer will suffer a loss in revenue as the vessel will not be able to operate by its intended date. Also, the buyer could be in breach of charterparty agreement with its ultimate clients. The question of whether the buyer could recover the loss suffered for such a breach from the shipbuilder will depend on whether such a claim is excluded under a consequential loss clause in the shipbuilding contract and the judicial construction of such a clause.

Thus, it is in the legal and financial interest of the shipbuilder and buyer to ensure that subcontractor's risk is suitably managed.

Shipbuilder's mitigation plan

While there is no absolute solution to subcontractors' risks, it could still be mitigated by a stringent pre-qualification and selection of subcontractors[209], close monitoring of their production process, and through suitable terms in the subcontract, as follows:

Battle of Form: All subcontracts must be based on the shipbuilder's standard form subcontract. Where the buyer requires a shipbuilder to subcontract a certain portion of the work to buyer's nominated subcontractors, a shipbuilder should only agree to contract with such nominated subcontractors upon the terms set out in shipbuilder's standard subcontract.

Effective Date of Contract: All of shipbuilder's subcontracts must provide that, if related shipbuilding contract; (a) is not effective within certain days of signing, or (b) is effective upon signing but subsequently becomes null and void because of condition

[209] *See sample Pre-Qualification Questionnaire, infra.*

subsequent; such subcontracts shall automatically become null and void, and the parties shall immediately and completely be discharged from all its obligations to each other under such subcontracts.

Scope of Work and Supply: All of subcontractor's work or supply should be free from defects in design, materials, and workmanship.

Warranty: The warranty period in all subcontracts should outlast those in related shipbuilding contracts. Such warranty must be assignable to the buyer. Subcontractors must provide warranty bond to secure its warranty obligations.

Subcontractor's Engineers: All subcontracts should provide that subcontractor's personnel deployed to provide any service for the shipbuilding project are competent and qualified in their respective craft or job skill with more than five years of relevant experience, certified medically fit by a licensed doctor. Such personnel must be in possession of safety certificates, valid passport and visa, work permit or employment pass required by government authorities of the country where the shipyard is located.

Shipbuilder shall be at liberty to require the subcontractor to replace any subcontractor's personnel found to be incompetent or neglectful in the performance of their duties or whose conduct is considered by shipbuilder to be undesirable. At the shipbuilder's request, the subcontractor shall, within a reasonable time, at its own costs replace any outgoing subcontractor' personnel with a substitute acceptable to shipbuilder.

Service Support: The subcontractor must maintain sufficient engineers to provide technical support services to the shipbuilder.

Suspension of Work: There shall be no suspension of subcontract work or supply on account of any disputes save where undisputed payment under any subcontract remains unpaid for 45 days.

Liquidated damages: The subcontract should provide that, save for permissible delay as defined in the subcontract, if the subcontractor fails to complete the subcontract work or deliver the equipment to the shipbuilder within the scheduled date stated in the subcontract, the subcontractor shall be liable to pay liquidated damages to the shipbuilder at a specified percentage of the subcontract price for each day or week of delay. Such liquidated damages shall be cap at 10% of the subcontract price.

Retention of Title: There shall be no retention of title to any equipment or materials supplied.

Liens and Encumbrances: There shall be no lien or encumbrances on the subcontract work and items supplied, regardless of whether such subcontract work is conducted at the shipyard or at subcontractor's worksite outside the shipyard.

Consequential Loss: The subcontract should define the meaning of "consequential loss" and provide that each party shall be responsible for their own consequential loss.

Reciprocal Indemnity: The subcontract must include a reciprocal indemnity provision for property damage or loss and personal injuries or death, regardless of the cause. Third-Party liability should be at law to the extent of the party's negligence.

Insurance: The subcontractor must provide workers' compensation, employer's liability insurance, and comprehensive general liability insurance (personal injury and property damage). Such insurance policies must be endorsed to include waivers of subrogation in favour of the shipbuilder group as defined in the subcontract.

Termination for Convenience: Where a related shipbuilding contract comprised a termination for convenience clause, the shipbuilder must have the right to end the subcontract for convenience.

Patent Indemnity: The subcontractor represents and warrants that all information and items whatsoever provided by the subcontractor to the shipbuilder is not in breach of any third-party intellectual property rights. The subcontractor shall indemnify, defend, and hold the shipbuilder harmless from any costs, expenses, damages, or liability that the shipbuilder may incur because of the subcontractor's contravention of this clause.

Intellectual Property: The subcontract must provide that intellectual property rights in all information or documents provided by shipbuilder to the subcontractor shall remain the sole and exclusive property of shipbuilder and/or its client or the actual owner as the case may be. The subcontractor shall indemnify, defend, and hold shipbuilder harmless from any costs, expenses (including legal fees), claims, damages, or liability that shipbuilder may incur from subcontractor's breach of this clause.

Confidentiality: All information, design, specification, drawings, plans, data, documents, and process furnished by the shipbuilder to the subcontractor (a) which are expressly marked as "confidential" or (b) if disclosed orally or visually, is reduced to writing, marked "confidential" and provided to the subcontractor within five (5) days of such disclosure, shall be deemed to be confidential information. The subcontractor shall not use the confidential information other

than in connection with the performance of the subcontract and shall always maintain the secrecy of such confidential information.
The subcontractor's obligation herein shall not apply to information which (a) is independently developed by the subcontractor and reduced into writing by the subcontractor before the date of the subcontract, (b) is generally available to the public other than through wrongful disclosure by the subcontractor, (c) is provided to the subcontractor by a third party lawfully and without a similar restriction on disclosure as contained herein, (d) the subcontractor is compelled by law to disclose.

Ethical Business Practice: Subcontractors or its employees, representatives and agents must comply with ethical business practice.

Health, Safety and Environment: The subcontract should provide that subcontractors and their personnel must comply with all health, safety, and environment requirements at the shipyard.

Additionally, and in respect of equipment supply, the subcontract must provide that;

- For international transactions, the shipping terms in the subcontract should be CIF, Incoterms, where the subcontractor is responsible for the costs, freight, and marine insurance to cover loss or damage to the equipment during transit.
- The equipment shall be (a) new and free from defects in design, materials, and workmanship, and (b) free from all liens, claims and encumbrances.
- The equipment must comply with the rules and regulations of the classification society and regulatory authorities, current on the date of the subcontract and those promulgated before such date

but which have a date for entry into force after the date of the subcontract.

- The equipment warranty period should be 18 months from the successfully completion of commissioning.
- Title to the equipment shall pass to the shipbuilder upon delivery and acceptance of the shipping documents.
- The subcontractor must ensure that its equipment will interface suitably with other equipment, system or appurtenant on the vessel. The subcontractor shall liaise directly with all related shipbuilder's subcontractors and classification society representatives working on the shipbuilding project to resolve any system interface issues expeditiously.
- Acceptance of the equipment shall occur when shipbuilder issues a completion certificate to confirm that all tests and trials of the equipment as required under the contract and specification have been duly completed to the satisfaction of the shipbuilder. For avoidance of doubt, shipbuilder's acceptance of the equipment shall not in any way diminished the subcontractor's obligations under the subcontract nor shall it constitute any acceptance by the shipbuilder of any responsibility for any defect in the equipment.

Buyer's mitigation plan

The buyer must conduct its own due diligence, vet, and approve all subcontractors proposed or nominated by the shipbuilder, inspect, attend all test and trials during the vessel's construction process.

Also, the shipbuilding contract should include a subcontractor's clause stating that the shipbuilder shall contract with subcontractors as principal and not as agent for the buyer, and the shipbuilder shall:

- Remain responsible for completion and delivery of the vessel.
- Ensure that its subcontractors comply with the provisions of the

main shipbuilding contract in the same way as if all the work is to be performed by the shipbuilder.

- Manage and supervise their subcontractor's activities.
- Warrant that all its subcontractors are paid timely.
- Indemnify and hold buyer harmless against payment default.
- Ensure that warranties in subcontracts are assignable to the buyer.
- Provide in all subcontracts, that shipbuilder's subcontractors shall not have any lien or retention of title rights over its work, services and items supplied to the vessel.

Pre-Qualification Questionnaire

ITEMS	REQUIRED DETAILS
Corporate Information	History, name, address, entity, nationality, former names, the parent company, subsidiaries, and affiliates.
Management	Names, experience, and qualifications.
Financial Data	Audited financial report for at the previous three years, plus unaudited quarterly financial report since last audited report.
Litigation	A list of all legal, arbitration and execution process filed against subcontractor during the past five years.
Liens	The number of liens filed against subcontractor during the past three years, the average and maximum values for those liens.
Cost Overruns	Subcontractor's claim for extra work that was disallowed by the counterparty or in arbitration or the courts.
Schedule Delays	The contract delivery dates and the actual completion dates for the last twelve most significant projects awarded to the subcontractor during the past three years.
Subcontractor Experience	Summary of work performed or equipment supplied by the subcontractor for shipyards and similar projects that would qualify the subcontractor for this project.
Factory Facilities	Factory location, layouts, covered work areas, manufacturing facilities and available space to fabricate the equipment.
Engineering	In-house engineering, planning, and scheduling capabilities.
Workloads	Number of personnel by crafts during the past 24 months, current staffing by crafts, and anticipated workloads during the calendar years of (year of intended work duration).
Health and Safety	The number of injuries, lost time accidents, fatalities, and total lost days for each of the past three years.
Quality Control	A summary of the subcontractor's quality assurance, control policy and procedures.
Statement of Qualification	Statement on why the subcontractor is well qualified to accomplish the project and customers' reference.

Shipbuilding and FPSO conversion

What is the different between shipbuilding and FPSO conversion?

Shipbuilding involves the construction of a new ship[210] from scratch. Such a ship may include bulk carrier, tanker ship, container ship, cruise ship, and offshore vessels like FPSO, FDPSO, drillship, jack-up, semi-submersible, platform supply vessel, anchor handling tugs, offshore construction and pipelay vessels, diving support vessel, and seismic survey ship. FPSO stands for a floating production storage and offloading vessel which is equipped with hydrocarbon processing equipment for separation and treatment of crude oil, water, and gases. It can be a new built vessel under a shipbuilding contract, or converted from an old tanker under an FPSO conversion contract.

---

[210] *The status of a ship or vessel is important for issues like tax, insurance, damages, personal injuries claim, maritime claim, and time limitation for legal proceeding. Some dictionary has defined a ship as a large boat used for carrying people or goods across the sea, a large spacecraft, or an aircraft. The Merchant Shipping Act of the UK provides that a "ship" includes every description of vessel used in navigation" In Halsbury's Laws, the meaning of "ship" reads: "Unless the context otherwise requires, 'ship' includes every description of vessel used in navigation. Whether a vessel comes within that meaning of a ship depends on the facts of each case; the statutory definition is intended to enlarge the meaning of "ship" To be a ship, a vessel must be used in navigable waters, either inland or at sea, and, although she must be constructed for navigation, it is not necessary to the definition that she should be able to navigate under her own power. The presence of a rudder and the manning of the vessel with a crew are important as showing that a vessel is a ship, but the absence of either does not mean that a vessel is not a ship. The purpose for which a vessel has been and is being used is also material when considering whether she is used in navigation."*

Shipbuilding

The shipyard is obligated to design, construct, equip and deliver a new vessel per the contract, specification, classification and regulatory rules and regulations, and all obligations set out in the contract. The shipyard's scope of work includes:

- Design, detailed engineering, shop drawings, as-built dossiers.
- Procurement of steel plates, sections, pipes, valves, fittings, deck outfitting, machineries, cranes, and propulsion auxiliaries; equipment related to electrical. instrumentation, telecoms, firefighting, safety, HVAC (heating, ventilation and air-conditioning), and navigation.
- Fabrication of the hull and superstructures.
- Shot-blasting and primer, steel cutting, and lay keel.
- Double bottom, blocks and deck house fabrication, blocks, and deck house erection.
- Piping fabrication and installation.
- Painting and outfitting.
- Launching of the vessel.
- Tests, precommissioning, and commissioning.
- Dockside, shipbuilders, and sea trials.
- Delivery of the vessel and issuance of delivery documents, certificates, and warranty bond.

The buyer may require a new vessel for its own use, or for speculation, sub-sale, or chartering purposes. The buyer is obligated under a shipbuilding contract to pay the contract price, provide payment guarantee and insurance, review and approve plans and drawings, approve subcontractors, inspect the work, attend tests and sea trials, and take delivery of the vessel.

FPSO conversion

Generally, the business case for an FPSO will arise from a series of contracts as follows:

- Production license/ share agreement between relevant Government Authority and Field Operators.
- FPSO lease agreement between Field Operators and FPSO Owner (or charterers).
- FPSO newbuild or conversion contract between FPSO Owner (or charterer) and Shipyard.

For FPSO conversion contract, the shipyard's scope of work will include modifications to the hull of an old tanker to extent life time, load bearing capacity, demolition, disposal of scraps and amongst others, the construction, upgrade, and installation of the following:

- Moon pool and pipe rack
- Drill pipe riser tensioner system
- Helideck support
- Marine piping systems
- Process plant and modules on the vessel's upper deck
- Power generation and distribution systems
- Ventilation and air conditioning systems
- Accommodation and facilities
- Drill pipe riser tensioner system

The FPSO owner will have to assess whether a specific tanker is suitable for conversion into an FPSO. This will include the evaluation of the tanker's structural integrity, capacity, and technical specifications of the tanker and field requirements. Thereafter, the owner's naval architects and marine engineers will have to develop detailed design and plans for the conversion. The FPSO owner is obligated under the conversion contract to pay the contract price, provide payment guarantee, insurance, review and approve plans and drawings, approve subcontractors, inspect the work, attend tests and sea trials, and take redelivery of the FPSO.

Shipbuilding and FPSO conversion contract

While the nature of a shipbuilding contract governed by English law is a contract for the sale of goods under the SOGA, an FPSO conversion contract is one for provision of work and materials under the Supply of Goods and Services Act 1982 and the Sale and Supply of Goods Act 1994.

While some of the contract terms in a shipbuilding and FPSO conversion may be similar, there are also differences.

Items	**Shipbuilding**	**FPSO Conversion**
Subject	New vessel built from scratch	Old tanker to FPSO. The tanker must arrive at the shipyard in a gas-free, and ready for hot work condition.
Parties	Shipyard and buyer	Shipyard and FPSO owner
Shipyard's Scope of Work	Design, build, equip and deliver new vessel	Hull modification, demolish, dismantle, repair, replace or upgrade with new items. More avenues for shipyard to create additional costs
Design Responsibility	Shipyard, save for buyer furnished equipment	Owner, save for items procured or furnished by shipyard

Items	**Shipbuilding**	**FPSO Conversion**
Contract Price	Fixed sum subject to adjustment for delays and variation	Lump sum and subject to adjustment for delays, variation, and remeasurement/MTO, providing ample opportunity for price increase and disputes
Variation	Variation mainly due to buyer's request and change in class rules	Unless the scope of work is defined comprehensively, ample opportunity for shipyard to submit variation requests
Test & Trials	Overall vessel's performance	Limited to work performed by shipyard
Delivery of the Vessel	Delivery	Redelivery
Defects Warranty	The vessel and appurtenant, excluding buyer's supplies	Limited to shipyard's scope of work and supply
Title	Title usually vests in shipyard till delivery of the vessel, and for remedies for payment default; see discussion under "Title to the Vessel"	Title remains with the owner at all times, thus remedies for payment default could include the arrest of the vessel
Crew	Required on board prior to delivery	Owner may deploy skeletal crew onboard during the conversion
Bunkering	Applicable during tests, trial, and delivery	Applicable from the tanker's arrival till redelivery

Statutes

INDEX

The author

The author is an erstwhile maritime lawyer, and in-house counsel for shipyard, subsea marine contractor, and owners of offshore vessels, pipelay vessels and FDPSO.

https://www.linkedin.com/in/seahdavid/

www.ingramcontent.com/pod-product-compliance
Lightning Source LLC
LaVergne TN
LVHW090318210926
848480LV00001B/283
* 9 7 9 8 2 2 3 7 9 3 1 7 5 *